Interfaces

A COMMUNICATIONS CASE BOOK FOR MENTAL HEALTH DECISION MAKERS

*By the
Committee on Mental Health Services
Group for the Advancement of Psychiatry*

Jossey-Bass Publishers
San Francisco • Washington • London • 1981

Published in association with
Mental Health Materials Center
Alex Sareyan, President

Library of Congress Cataloging in Publication Data

Interfaces: a communications case book for mental health decision makers.

    1. Communication in psychiatry—Case studies. 2. Psychiatry—Decision making—Case studies. 3. Psychiatric consultation—Case studies. I. Group for the Advancement of Psychiatry. Committee on Mental Health Services.
RC437.2.IVV   616.89   81-9551
ISBN 0-87589-510-7   AACR2

Copyright © 1981 by the Mental Health Materials Center. All rights reserved. This report must not be reproduced in any form without written permission of the Mental Health Materials Center, except by a reviewer, reporter, or commentator who wishes to quote brief passages.

Volume XI, Publication No. 107.

This is the first in a series of publications comprising Volume XI.

Copies of this publication are available from
Jossey Bass Inc., Publishers
433 California Street
San Francisco, California 94104
for the United States and Possessions, and for Canada, Australia, New Zealand, and Japan.
Copies for the rest of the world are available from
Jossey-Bass Limited
28 Banner Street
London EClY 8QE

Manufactured in the United States of America

JACKET DESIGN BY WILLI BAUM

FIRST EDITION

Code 8124

CONTENTS

    Statement of Purpose 5
    Committee Acknowledgments 11
    Publisher's Foreword 12

1. Introduction 13
2. Interface I: The Police Officer 17
3. Interface II: The Patient Advocate 39
4. Interface III: The Third-Party Payor 55
5. Interface IV: The Non-Psychiatric Physician 77
6. Interface V: The Health Planner 99
7. Interface VI: The Budget Analyst 119
8. Interface VII: The Legislator 137
9. Conclusion 157

    Acknowledgments to Contributors 164
    Index 165

STATEMENT OF PURPOSE

THE GROUP FOR THE ADVANCEMENT OF PSYCHIATRY has a membership of approximately 300 psychiatrists, most of whom are organized in the form of a number of working committees. These committees direct their efforts toward the study of various aspects of psychiatry and the application of this knowledge to the fields of mental health and human relations.

Collaboration with specialists in other disciplines has been and is one of GAP's working principles. Since the formation of GAP in 1946 its members have worked closely with such other specialists as anthropologists, biologists, economists, statisticians, educators, lawyers, nurses, psychologists, sociologists, social workers, and experts in mass communication, philosophy, and semantics. GAP envisages a continuing program of work according to the following aims:

1. To collect and appraise significant data in the fields of psychiatry, mental health, and human relations
2. To reevaluate old concepts and to develop and test new ones
3. To apply the knowledge thus obtained for the promotion of mental health and good human relations

GAP is an independent group, and its reports represent the composite findings and opinions of its members only, guided by its many consultants.

INTERFACES: A COMMUNICATIONS CASE BOOK FOR MENTAL HEALTH DECISION MAKERS was formulated by the Committee on Mental Health Services, which acknowledges on page 11 the participation of others in the preparation of this report. The members of this committee are listed below. The following pages list the members of the other GAP committees as well as additional membership categories and current and past officers of GAP.

COMMITTEE ON MENTAL HEALTH SERVICES

Allan Beigel, Tucson, AZ,
  Chairperson
Mary Ann B. Bartusis, Morrisville, PA
Eugene M. Caffey, Jr., Bowie, MD
Merrill T. Eaton, Omaha, NB
Joseph T. English, New York, NY
James Funkhouser, Richmond, VA
W. Walter Menninger, Topeka, KS
Jose Maria Santiago, Tucson, AZ
Donald J. Scherl, Boston, MA
Herzl R. Spiro, Milwaukee, WI
George F. Wilson, Belle Mead, NJ
Jack A. Wolford, Pittsburgh, PA

COMMITTEE ON ADOLESCENCE

Warren J. Gadpaille, Englewood, CO,
  Chairperson
Ian A. Canino, New York, NY
Harrison P. Eddy, New York, NY
Sherman C. Feinstein, Highland Park, IL
Maurice R. Friend, New York, NY
Michael Kalogerakis, New York, NY
Clarice J. Kestenbaum, New York, NY
Derek Miller, Chicago, IL
Silvio J. Onesti, Jr., Belmont, MA

COMMITTEE ON AGING

Charles M. Gaitz, Houston, TX,
  Chairperson
Gene D. Cohen, Rockville, MD
Lawrence F. Greenleigh, Los Angeles, CA
Maurice E. Linden, Philadelphia, PA
Eric Pfeiffer, Tampa, FL
George H. Pollock, Chicago, IL
Harvey Ruben, New Haven, CT
F. Conyers Thompson, Jr., Atlanta, GA
Jack Weinberg, Chicago, IL

COMMITTEE ON CHILD PSYCHIATRY

John F. McDermott, Jr., Honolulu, HI,
  Chairperson
Paul L. Adams, Louisville, KY
E. James Anthony, St. Louis, MO
James M. Bell, Canaan, NY
Harlow Donald Dunton, New York, NY

Joseph Fischhoff, Detroit, MI
Joseph M. Green, Madison, WI
Theodore Shapiro, New York, NY
*Exie E. Welsch, New York, NY

COMMITTEE ON THE COLLEGE STUDENT

Robert L. Arnstein, Hamden, CT,
  Chairperson
Varda Backus, La Jolla, CA
Myron B. Liptzin, Chapel Hill, NC
Malkah Tolpin Notman, Brookline, MA
Gloria C. Onque, Pittsburgh, PA
Elizabeth Aub Reid, Cambridge, MA
Kent E. Robinson, Towson, MD
Earle Silber, Chevy Chase, MD

COMMITTEE ON CULTURAL PSYCHIATRY

Andrea K. Delgado, New York, NY,
  Chairperson
Ronald M. Wintrob, Farmington, CT

COMMITTEE ON THE FAMILY

Henry U. Grunebaum, Cambridge, MA,
  Chairperson
W. Robert Beavers, Dallas, TX
Ivan Boszormenyi-Nagy, Wyncote, PA
Lee Combrinck-Graham, Philadelphia, PA
Ira D. Glick, New York, NY
Frederick Gottlieb, Los Angeles, CA
Charles A. Malone, Cleveland, OH
David Mendell, Houston, TX
Norman L. Paul, Boston, MA
Joseph Satten, San Francisco, CA

COMMITTEE ON GOVERNMENTAL AGENCIES

Sidney S. Goldensohn, Jamaica, NY,
  Chairperson
James P. Cattell, Monterey, MA
Naomi Heller, Washington, DC
Roger Peele, Washington, DC
William W. Van Stone, Palo Alto, CA
William D. Weitzel, Lexington, KY

*deceased

COMMITTEE ON HANDICAPS

Norman R. Bernstein, Chicago, IL,
  Chairperson
Betty J. Pfefferbaum, Houston, TX
George Tarjan, Los Angeles, CA
Thomas G. Webster, Washington, DC
Henry H. Work, Washington, DC

COMMITTEE ON INTERNATIONAL RELATIONS

Francis F. Barnes, Chevy Chase, MD,
  Chairperson
Robert M. Dorn, Norfolk, VA
John E. Mack, Chestnut Hill, MA
Rita R. Rogers, Torrance, CA
Bertram H. Schaffner, New York, NY
Stephen B. Shanfield, Tucson, AZ
Vamik D. Volkan, Charlottesville, VA
Roy M. Whitman, Cincinnati, OH

COMMITTEE ON MEDICAL EDUCATION

David R. Hawkins, Chicago, IL,
  Chairperson
Carol Nadelson, Boston, MA
Herbert Pardes, Rockville, MD
Carolyn R. Robinowitz, Bethesda, MD
Jeanne Spurlock, Washington, DC
Bryce Templeton, Philadelphia, PA
Sidney L. Werkman, Denver, CO
Paul Tyler Wilson, Bethesda, MD
Sherwyn M. Woods, Los Angeles, CA

COMMITTEE ON PREVENTIVE PSYCHIATRY

Stephen Fleck, New Haven, CT,
  Chairperson
C. Knight Aldrich, Charlottesville, VA
Viola Bernard, New York, NY
Jules V. Coleman, New Haven, CT
William H. Hetznecker, Philadelphia, PA
Richard G. Morrill, Boston, MA
Harris B. Peck, New Rochelle, NY

COMMITTEE ON PSYCHIATRY AND COMMUNITY

John J. Schwab, Louisville, KY,
  Chairperson
John C. Nemiah, Boston, MA

Alexander S. Rogawski, Los Angeles, CA
John A. Talbott, New York, NY
Charles B. Wilkinson, Kansas City, MO

COMMITTEE ON PSYCHIATRY AND LAW

Loren H. Roth, Pittsburgh, PA,
  Chairperson
Edward T. Auer, Bryn Mawr, PA
Elissa P. Benedek, Ann Arbor, MI
Park E. Dietz, Belmont, MA
John Donnelly, Hartford, CT
Seymour L. Halleck, Chapel Hill, NC
Carl P. Malmquist, Minneapolis, MN
A. Louis McGarry, Great Neck, NY
Herbert C. Modlin, Topeka, KS
Jonas R. Rappeport, Baltimore, MD

COMMITTEE ON PSYCHIATRY AND RELIGION

Albert J. Lubin, Woodside, CA,
  Chairperson
Sidney S. Furst, Bronx, NY
Richard C. Lewis, New Haven, CT
Mortimer Ostow, Bronx, NY
Clyde R. Snyder, Columbus, MO
Michael R. Zales, Greenwich, CT

COMMITTEE ON PSYCHIATRY IN INDUSTRY

Duane Q. Hagen, St. Louis, MO,
  Chairperson
Barrie S. Greiff, Boston, MA
R. Edward Huffman, Asheville, NC
Herbert L. Klemme, Stillwater, MN
Alan A. McLean, New York, NY
David E. Morrison, Palatine, NY
Clarence J. Rowe, St. Paul, MN
John Wakefield, Saratoga, CA

COMMITTEE ON PSYCHOPATHOLOGY

David A. Adler, Boston, MA,
  Chairperson
Eric A. Baum, Akron, OH
Wagner H. Bridger, Bronx, NY
Doyle I. Carson, Dallas, TX
Paul E. Huston, Iowa City, IA
Richard E. Renneker, Los Angeles, CA

COMMITTEE ON PUBLIC EDUCATION

Robert J. Campbell, New York, NY,
  Chairperson
Norman L. Loux, Sellersville, PA
Mildred Mitchell-Bateman, Huntington, WV
Julius Schreiber, Washington, DC
Miles F. Shore, Boston, MA
Robert A. Solow, Beverly Hills, CA
Kent A. Zimmerman, Berkeley, CA

COMMITTEE ON RESEARCH

Jerry M. Lewis, Dallas, TX,
  Chairperson
John E. Adams, Gainesville, FL
Robert Cancro, New York, NY
Stanley H. Eldred, Belmont, MA
John G. Gunderson, Belmont, MA
Morris A. Lipton, Chapel Hill, NC
John G. Looney, Dallas, TX
Charles P. O'Brien, Philadelphia, PA
Alfred H. Stanton, Wellesley Hills, MA
John S. Strauss, New Haven, CT

COMMITTEE ON SOCIAL ISSUES

Roy W. Menninger, Topeka, KS,
  Chairperson
Henry J. Gault, Highland Park, IL
Roderic Gorney, Los Angeles, CA
Perry Ottenberg, Philadelphia, PA

COMMITTEE ON THERAPEUTIC CARE

Orlando B. Lightfoot, Boston, MA,
  Chairperson
Bernard Bandler, Cambridge, MA
Thomas E. Curtis, Chapel Hill, NC
Robert W. Gibson, Towson, MD
Donald W. Hammersley, Washington, DC
Roberto L. Jimenez, San Antonio, TX
Milton Kramer, Cincinnati, OH
Melvin Sabshin, Washington, DC

COMMITTEE ON THERAPY

Robert Michels, New York, NY,
  Chairperson
Henry W. Brosin, Tucson, AZ
Eugene B. Feigelson, Brooklyn, NY

Tokoz Byram Karasu, New York, NY
Andrew P. Morrison, Cambridge, MA
William C. Offenkrantz, Milwaukee, WI
Lewis L. Robbins, Glen Oaks, NY
Allan D. Rosenblatt, La Jolla, CA

CONTRIBUTING MEMBERS

Carlos C. Alden, Jr., Buffalo, NY
E. James Anthony, St. Louis, MO
Charlotte G. Babcock, Port Charlotte, FL
Howard V. Bair, Colorado Springs, CO
Grace Baker, New York, NY
Spencer Bayles, Houston, TX
Aaron T. Beck, Wynnewood, PA
C. Christian Beels, New York, NY
Sidney Berman, Washington, DC
Wilfred Bloomberg, Cambridge, MA
Thomas L. Brannick, Imola, CA
H. Keith H. Brodie, Durham, NC
C. Martel Bryant, San Francisco, CA
Ewald W. Busse, Durham, NC
Robert N. Butler, Washington, DC

Paul Chodoff, Washington, DC
Ian L. W. Clancy, Ontario, Canada
Sanford I. Cohen, Boston, MA

William D. Davidson, Washington, DC
Robert W. Dorn, Norfolk, VA

Lloyd C. Elam, Nashville, TN
Louis C. English, Pomona, NY

Raymond Feldman, Boulder, CO
Stuart M. Finch, Tucson, AZ
Alfred Flarsheim, Wilmette, IL
Archie R. Foley, New York, NY
Alan Frank, Albuquerque, NM
Daniel X. Freedman, Chicago, IL
James B. Funkhouser, Richmond, VA

Robert S. Garber, Belle Mead, NJ
Albert J. Glass, Bethesda, MD
Louis A. Gottschalk, Irvine, CA
Alexander Gralnick, Port Chester, NY
Harold A. Greenberg, Silver Spring, MD
Milton Greenblatt, Los Angeles, CA
*Maurice H. Greenhill, Rye, NY

* Deceased

John H. Greist, Indianapolis, IN
Roy R. Grinker, Sr., Chicago, IL
Lester Grinspoon, Boston, MA
Ernest M. Gruenberg, Baltimore, MD

Stanley Hammons, Lexington, KY
Joel S. Handler, Wilmette, IL
Saul I. Harrison, Ann Arbor, MI
Peter Hartocollis, Topeka, KS
J. Cotter Hirshberg, Topeka, KS
Edward J. Hornick, New York, NY
Joseph Hughes, Philadelphia, PA
Portia Bell Hume, St. Helena, CA

Benjamin Jeffries, Harper Woods, MI

Jay Katz, New Haven, CT
Sheppard G. Kellam, Chicago, IL
Donald F. Klein, New York, NY
Gerald L. Klerman, Cambridge, MA
Peter H. Knapp, Boston, MA
James A. Knight, New Orleans, LA
Othilda M. Krug, Cincinnati, OH

Robert L. Leopold, Philadelphia, PA
Alan I. Levenson, Tucson, AZ
Ruth W. Lidz, Woodbridge, CT
Earl A. Loomis, Jr., Greenport, NY
Reginald S. Lourie, Chevy Chase, MD
Alfred O. Ludwig, Boston, MA

Jeptha R. MacFarlane, Garden City, NY
John A. MacLeod, Cincinnati, OH
Leo Madow, Philadelphia, PA
Peter A. Martin, Southfield, MI
Ake Mattsson, New York, NY
David Mendell, Houston, TX
Mary E. Mercer, Nyack, NY
Eugene Meyer, Baltimore, MD
James G. Miller, Louisville, KY
David F. Musto, New Haven, CT

John E. Nardini, Washington, DC
Joseph D. Noshpitz, Washington, DC

Lucy D. Ozarin, Bethesda, MD

Bernard L. Pacella, New York, NY
Norman L. Paul, Boston, MA
Marvin E. Perkins, Roanoke, VA
Charles A. Pinderhughes, Bedford, MA
Seymour Pollack, Los Angeles, CA

David N. Ratnavale, Bethesda, MD
Walter Reich, Rockville, MD
Harvey L. P. Resnik, College Park, MD
W. Donald Ross, Cincinnati, OH
Lester H. Rudy, Chicago, IL
George E. Ruff, Philadelphia, PA
A. John Rush, Dallas, TX

David S. Sanders, Los Angeles, CA
Kurt O. Schlesinger, San Francisco, CA
Robert A. Senescu, Albuquerque, NM
Calvin F. Settlage, Sausalito, CA
Richard I. Shader, Newton Centre, MA
Charles Shagass, Philadelphia, PA
Harley C. Shands, New York, NY
Albert J. Silverman, Ann Arbor, MI
Justin Simon, Berkeley, CA
Kendon W. Smith, Valhalla, NY
Benson R. Snyder, Cambridge, MA
David A. Soskis, Bala Cynwyd, PA
John F. Spiegel, Waltham, MA
Tom G. Stauffer, White Plains, NY
Brandt F. Steele, Denver, CO
Eleanor A. Steele, Denver, CO
Rutherford B. Stevens, New York, NY
Alan A. Stone, Cambridge, MA
Robert E. Switzer, Trevose, PA

Perry C. Talkington, Dallas, TX
Graham C. Taylor, Montreal, Canada
Prescott W. Thompson, Beaverton, OR
Harvey J. Tompkins, New York, NY
Lucia E. Tower, Chicago, IL
Joseph P. Tupin, Sacramento, CA
John A. Turner, San Francisco, CA

Montague Ullman, Ardsley, NY
Gene L. Usdin, New Orleans, LA

Warren T. Vaughan, Jr., Portola Valley, CA

Robert S. Wallerstein, San Francisco, CA
Andrew S. Watson, Ann Arbor, MI
Bryant M. Wedge, Washington, DC
Joseph B. Wheelwright, Kentfield, CA
Robert L. Williams, Houston, TX

Stanley F. Yolles, Stony Brook, NY

Israel Zwerling, Philadelphia, PA

LIFE MEMBERS

S. Spafford Ackerly, Louisville, KY
C. Knight Aldrich, Charlottesville, VA
Bernard Bandler, Cambridge, MA
Leo H. Bartemeier, Baltimore, MD
Walter E. Barton, Hartland, VT
Ivan C. Berlien, Coral Gables, FL
Murray Bowen, Chevy Chase, MD
O. Spurgeon English, Narberth, PA
Dana L. Farnsworth, Belmont, MA
Stephen Fleck, New Haven, CT
Jerome Frank, Baltimore, MD
Edward O. Harper, Cleveland, OH
Margaret M. Lawrence, Pomona, NY
Harold I. Lief, Philadelphia, PA
Judd Marmor, Los Angeles, CA
Karl A. Menninger, Topeka, KS
Lewis L. Robbins, Glen Oaks, NY
Mabel Ross, Sun City, AZ
*Benjamin Simon, Boston, MA
Francis A. Sleeper, Cape Elizabeth, ME

LIFE CONSULTANT

Mrs. Ethel L. Ginsburg, New York, NY

BOARD OF DIRECTORS

OFFICERS

President

Jack Weinberg
1601 West Taylor Street
Chicago, Il 60612

President-Elect

Henry H. Work
1700 Eighteenth Street, N.W.
Washington, DC 20009

Secretary

Allan Beigel
30 Camino Espanole
Tucson, AZ 85716

---

* Deceased

Treasurer

Michael R. Zales
Edgewood Drive
Greenwich, CT 06830

Immediate Past President, 1979-81

Robert W. Gibson
Sheppard and Enoch Pratt Hospital
Towson, MD 21204

Board Members

Donald W. Hammersley
Malkah Tolpin Notman
William C. Offenkrantz
Ronald M. Wintrob

Past Presidents

*William C. Menninger	1946-51
Jack R. Ewalt	1951-53
Walter E. Barton	1953-55
*Sol W. Ginsburg	1955-57
Dana L. Farnsworth	1957-59
*Marion E. Kenworthy	1959-61
Henry W. Brosin	1961-63
Leo H. Bartemeier	1963-65
Robert S. Garber	1965-67
Herbert C. Modlin	1967-69
John Donnelly	1969-71
George Tarjan	1971-73
Judd Marmor	1973-75
John C. Nemiah	1975-77
Jack A. Wolford	1977-79

PUBLICATIONS BOARD

Chairman

Merrill T. Eaton
Nebraska Psychiatric Institute
602 South 45th Street
Omaha, NB 68106

C. Knight Aldrich
Warren Gadpaille
Carl P. Malmquist
Perty Ottenberg
Carolyn B. Robinowitz
Alexander S. Rogawski

Consultant
John C. Nemiah

Ex-Officio
Jack Weinberg
Henry H. Work

Committee Acknowledgments

The Committee on Mental Health Services was under the Chairmanship of Allan Beigel, when this report was formulated.

At that time, the Committee also included the following members of the Group for the Advancement of Psychiatry: Mary Ann Bartusis, Eugene M. Caffey, Jr., Merrill T. Eaton, Joseph T. English, James Funkhouser, Robert S. Garber, W. Walter Menninger, Jose Santiago, Donald J. Scherl, Herzl Spiro, George F. Wilson, and Jack Wolford.

Drs. Funkhouser and Garber are now contributing rather than active members of GAP. The current Chairman of the Committee on Mental Health Services is Dr. Spiro.

The Committee wishes to express its appreciation to two GAP Fellows who aided in the formulation of this report: Drs. Sharon Jaynes and Emmett M. Lampkin.

The Committee benefitted immeasurably from the editorial assistance of George Hough and from the consultation and support of Edward F.X. Lawlor, Jr. and Ms. Irene Lump.

Finally, the many psychiatrists and decision-makers in other fields who assisted in the preparation of this report are listed at the beginning of each chapter. To all, we extend our thanks for their able assistance.

Allan Beigel

THE JOSSEY-BASS SERIES
IN SOCIAL AND BEHAVIORAL SCIENCES

PUBLISHER'S FOREWORD

We are pleased to publish this important book by the Group for the Advancement of Psychiatry. It calls attention to the need for better communication between mental health professionals and others involved in decisions about mental health issues.

Today, mental health professionals are frequently called upon to interact with a wide range of groups outside the mental health field in providing the best possible care to their clients. Many mental health professionals, unaccustomed to presenting clients' needs to such groups as lawyers, police officers, and social workers, feel the need for assistance in collaborating with these various groups in a productive, mutually beneficial way. This book fills that need by illustrating many of the communication problems experienced and by suggesting how better understanding and cooperation can be achieved.

Although the psychiatrist is the professional portrayed in these dialogues, the interaction discussed could apply equally well to a social worker, psychologist, counselor, family therapist, or other mental health professional.

We are grateful to the Mental Health Materials Center and its president, Alex Sareyan, for their timely work on the manuscript and to the Committee on Mental Health Services of the Group for the Advancement of Psychiatry for the study.

Allen Jossey-Bass

1

INTRODUCTION

In the past thirty years, public concern has prompted the creation of two national commissions on mental health as well as widespread state and local citizen interest and activity. The courts have vigorously expressed community expectations; legislatures have restructured commitment and other mental health laws; and services for the emotionally disturbed have become more available through increased public funding and coverage by an increasing number of health insurance programs.

In one generation, psychiatrists and other mental health professionals have become aware that they no longer can be isolationists, and that they must communicate with an array of "publics." Fellow physicians seek effective liaison about patient problems, while lawyers are concerned with defining patients' rights in contrast to psychiatrists' emphasis on patients' needs. Psychiatrists solicit support for mental health services from public health planning agencies, government budget analysts, and legislators. Third-party payors, public and private, look to the psychiatrist for evidence that what is provided for patients is required for their improvement.

These changes have occurred with explosive speed and many psychiatrists have been ill-prepared to deal effectively with such a variety of persons and groups. Their education has emphasized dealing quietly and confidentially with their patients within the traditional physician-patient relationship, applying biopsychosocial concepts to the treatment of mental illness. They have had little opportunity to test their interpersonal skills with caregivers outside of the mental health field.

However, today, the psychiatrist is being called upon increasingly to present the needs of his patients to persons and groups who do not provide direct services to the emotionally disturbed. As a result, psychiatrists often feel "de-skilled" because they are unfamiliar with the natures and needs of these other publics. Not well-trained to be public advocates, psychiatrists are seldom skilled in rhetoric, well informed about administrative principles, expert in sales techniques, or talented in politics.

The members of the Committee on Mental Health Services began the preparation of this Manual by sharing their experiences, successful and frustrating, at many interfaces which impact on their professional activities. They perceived the need for a manual, handbook or set of guidelines illustrative of some of the communication problems, with the many groups with which the psychiatrist must interact as he provides care to patients.

This publication seeks to stimulate discussion around real situations by highlighting some of the inevitable imperfections in performance of both parties to the dialogue, by providing commentaries by psychiatrists and those with whom they collaborate, and by outlining some measures which might improve mutual understanding. It does not undertake to explore, extensively or intensively, the literature of administration and management concerned with the areas covered.

The process used to develop this publication began with an informal survey of approximately three dozen apparent "adversaries" in the daily skirmishes. Who could describe better to the Committee the difficulties in understanding psychiatry and its practitioners? Representatives of many of the publics were asked, "What questions are not answered to your satisfaction by mental health professions?"

Introduction 15

A police chief replied, "Why won't psychiatrists give me a straight answer when I want to know about the condition of a prisoner or someone we have just arrested?" An insurance reviewer commented, "Generally speaking, when insurance company representatives speak with psychiatrists, they are confronted with silence, suspicion, and the withholding of information. The confidentiality rules, as well as privacy legislation, have made dealing with them very difficult." A clergyman wondered, "Do psychiatrists have difficulty in accepting clergy as counselors in their own right?" A state budget analyst challenged, "How can we know money put into mental health treatment is money well spent?" The non-psychiatrists' doubts about psychiatry and psychiatrists clearly indicate the presence of communication problems.

To clarify the issues further, the Commitee prepared seven vignettes to illustrate some of the common areas of difficulty. The sketches were submitted to a panel of approximately fifty psychiatrists and non-psychiatrists who make decisions about the mentally ill. Their reviews were summarized with special attention to the identified contributions to misunderstanding made by participants on either side of the interface.

These dialogues, with associated points of view and discussions, may provoke in readers wry reminiscence or outright disagreement. Although they are derived from real occurrences, they are deliberately overdrawn to make the communication problems unmistakable. They are intended to be vehicles for consideration of the obstacles to understanding which occur in such situations. Decision-making in the mental health field now involves a wide range of persons from different educational backgrounds, so mutual understanding of the issues is initially difficult. Specific outcomes will, of course, depend upon local attitudes, circumstances, levels of persuasive and professional skills among the participants, available time, constraints by parent organizations, and many other factors. These examples and analyses, however, should lead to understandings through which better communication between psychiatrists and decision-makers in other public areas can be attained.

Because this document is the product of a group of psychiatrists, the mental health professionals we have portrayed are psychiatrists. Nevertheless, we believe that much of this report is relevant to the other "helping professions" who frequently must grapple with similar situations.

2

**INTERFACE I
THE POLICE OFFICER**

Acknowledgments

We gratefully acknowledge the assistance of the following in the preparation of this chapter:

Samuel J. Gemelli, *Chief of Police, Erie PA*

Patrick E. Kelly, *Legal Advisor, Tucson Police Department, Tucson AZ*

Herbert C. Modlin, *Professor of Forensic Psychiatry, Menninger Foundation, Topeka KS*

Jonas B. Rappeport, *Chief Medical Officer, Supreme Bench of Baltimore, Baltimore MD*

Robert L. Sadoff, *Associate Clinical Professor of Psychiatry, University of Pennsylvania; Lecturer in Law, Villanova University School of Law, Philadelphia PA*

Alan A. Stone, *Professor of Law and Psychiatry, Harvard University, Cambridge MA*

2

Interface I

The Police Officer

DIALOGUE

SETTING: The following dialogue takes place late on a Saturday evening in the admission lobby of a 400-bed state hospital that provides psychiatric services to both children and adults. Its 31-county catchment area has a population of 1.5 million citizens and encompasses both rural and urban areas. Some of the counties offer inpatient psychiatric services as part of comprehensive community mental health centers; others do not.

Law enforcement personnel have the option of bringing an individual who is apparently emotionally ill to the hospital for emergency admission when the probate court* is not open. The state law allows for up to 48 hours (or until the court has been open for 48 hours). Such hospitalization requires application by a police officer and agreement/acceptance by an admitting physician at the state hospital. If the physician does not agree that the person is emotionally ill and dangerous beyond a reasonable doubt, he may refuse admission.

---

* Courts in different states may use a department different from that used in this dialogue.

PARTICIPANTS: Officer Peters—Police Officer
Officer Allen—Police Officer
Dr. Barry—Emergency Room Psychiatrist
Mrs. Smith—Local Citizen
Mrs. Jones—Prospective Patient

SCENE 1

At 10:00 p.m. Officers Peters and Allen, local police patrolmen, bring Mrs. Jones to the hospital for admission. They are greeted in the lobby by Dr. Barry, the psychiatrist on duty. Officer Peters talks to Dr. Barry while Officer Allen remains with Mrs. Jones.

Dr. Barry: What seems to be the problem?

Officer Peters: Well, Doc, we got a call from some neighbors of this woman. They said she was behaving strangely and they were afraid she was going to set fire to her house. The neighbors told us she had been out in the back yard dousing some metal bedsprings with gasoline and setting them on fire. She was doing this near the wooden fence which separates her house from a next-door neighbor who had been outside with his hose to make sure the flames didn't spread.

When we rang the doorbell, she seemed a little "hyper." She asked what we wanted and told us she didn't think that there was anything wrong with what she was doing. She let us in, and her place was really a shambles. It looked like someone had gone absoutely berserk; furniture was broken and things were thrown all over. She didn't seem to make much sense, either, so we thought we ought to bring her here.

Dr. Barry: Is there anything else I ought to know?

The Police Officer

Officer Peters: Well, ... the neighbors said she had been doing lots of strange things lately. Apparently she has a drinking problem and her husband left her because she wouldn't get help for that. We were told that she's been at the VA Hospital in their alcohol program but that she won't go back there. Ever since her husband left her, she's been a real "weirdo." Her neighbors say she goes around the house nude with the window shades up; she even greeted the gas meter reader that way! And they're afraid of what she might do to them for reporting her. She seems to be unstable.

Dr. Barry: All right, Officer. I'll talk to her and see what I can learn. May I ask you to wait a few minutes?

Officer Peters: Okay, but I hope it doesn't take too long, Doc. We have to answer some other calls.

SCENE II

Dr. Barry visits Mrs. Jones and discovers that she is 56, a former military nurse who is able to give a fairly intelligible history of her drinking problem and her hospitalization for treatment at the local VA hospital. When she felt she no longer needed treatment she left against the advice of the program personnel. She admits she still does some drinking; that her husband left her because he thought she ought to get more help; that she is upset about his leaving and doesn't know what she can do about it. She is unhappy, but she does not feel she is sick or needs hospitalization or treatment.

With regard to the incident which brought the police to her house, she reported in a matter-of-fact manner that she was concerned about bedbugs. She recalled a time when the military took care of a bedbug problem by burning the springs; so she dragged her bedsprings out into the back yard and was *doing just that. She knew what she was doing and felt everything was under control. Besides, her neighbor was ready with his hose in case anything went wrong.*

In the interview, she seemed to ramble a bit, but was well oriented and alert. She responded respectfully to the psychiatrist, but made it clear that she would not stay in the hospital willingly. She had things to do at home. She was a little agitated, but said she would be willing to come to the outpatient clinic to talk to someone on Monday morning.

Dr. Barry then goes back to talk with Officer Peters.

Dr. Barry: Officer, I've talked with Mrs. Jones. She seems a bit agitated and it appears she has some emotional problems, but I think she knows what she's doing. And as you know, to be hospitalized involuntarily, a person must be considered dangerous beyond a reasonable doubt. My impression is that she knows what she did was a bit risky, but she seems rational now. I see no evidence that she's actually intoxicated, and even if she were, this wouldn't be the place for her. She says she does not think she needs help. I don't think the problems she has are sufficiently severe for her being held here involuntarily. The judge is likely to release her at the "probable cause hearing" Monday anyway.

Officer Peters: But Doc, if you saw her house, you'd know she's bonkers. It was a mess! And the way she was drenching things with gasoline—the fumes were something else.

Dr. Barry: As you know, Officer Peters, our Probate Judge is a strict constructionist. The law says a person must be dangerous to self or others, "beyond a reasonable doubt," to be held against his will. Destruction of one's own property doesn't count. She's promised she won't try to burn the bedbugs off the springs any more, and that she'll come to the outpatient clinic on Monday.

Officer Peters: Doc, I wish you would talk to the neighbors. They've been keeping an eye on her for several days and they are really worried. In fact, they're afraid of her.

Dr. Barry: Well, I don't doubt that. I'm sure she has the potential for some strange behavior. But I don't know how dangerous it is to walk around nude with the shades up. That kind of behavior may be a public nuisance, but knowing how the judge has responded to other similar actions, I'm sure she'll dismiss Mrs. Jones.

Officer Peters: But Doc, what are we supposed to do with this woman? The folks asked us to keep the peace, and she was certainly disturbing the neighorhood. She wasn't using very good judgment, and you expect us to take her back there. She doesn't belong in jail—you can see that. Couldn't you just go ahead and hold her over the weekend? So what if the judge turns her loose on Monday? Whatever she has will be better by then.

Dr. Barry: Well, I really don't think that's right; it's manipulating the law. She's already settled down a bit. I don't think she's likely to be a problem any more tonight or tomorrow—it's already had an impact on her. I wish we had a better solution, but I just can't justify admitting her. We're tight on beds anyway, and we've been told to put the lid on unnecessary after-hours admissions.

Officer Peters: For Christ's sake, Doc, how are we going to explain that to the folks who live next door? I don't want to put people away any more than you do, but I don't think she can stay home right now. . . . I've got to call my supervisor.

SCENE III

Officer Peters has called his supervising Lieutenant and rejoins Dr. Barry.

Officer Peters: Doc, I wish you'd either talk to my Lieutenant or to a next-door neighbor of Mrs. Jones who called him asking whether Mrs. Jones is going to be admitted to the hospital. She's afraid Mrs. Jones knows she's the one that called the police, and she's afraid of some kind of retaliation. She's afraid to go to sleep tonight until she knows what's going to happen. Could you maybe call her and reconsider your decision?

Dr. Barry: Well, all right.

SCENE IV

Dr. Barry calls Mrs. Smith, Mrs. Jones's next-door neighbor.

Dr. Barry: Mrs. Smith? This is Dr. Barry at Parkview Hospital. I understand you are concerned about Mrs. Jones. Could you tell me what you know about the problem?

Mrs. Smith: Doctor, she's really been upset lately. Ever since her husband left her, she's been up all hours of the night. She's been breaking things up—furniture and the like—in her home. She doesn't pull down her shades. She's unpredictable. She drinks a lot. And I don't know what she's likely to do. I've got two small children and I'm afraid she may do something to hurt them. I'm sure she knows I called the police, and I'm afraid she'll hold that against me. She was doing crazy things today, dousing gasoline on the bedsprings and setting them on fire. If the neighbor on the other side hadn't been there with his hose, I don't know what might have happened.

Dr. Barry: Did the fence actually catch fire?

Mrs. Smith: No, but it could have. She certainly wasn't really watching the fire very closely . . . and our houses are close together too, Doctor.

Dr. Barry: Well, I can appreciate your concern, Mrs. Smith, but at this point Mrs. Jones seems to have settled down and she feels she'll be all right. She isn't acting in a way now that I would consider dangerous to herself or others.

Mrs. Smith: Maybe not right now, Doctor. But she's not stable. I'm really worried about what might happen if she comes back home tonight. Can't you keep her there, at least for tonight? She certainly needs some kind of help.

Dr. Barry: Well, I don't know . . . I'll talk with Mrs. Jones again. I can't promise anything, but I do understand your worry. However, I don't think, from talking with Mrs. Jones, that she has bad feelings toward you, or that she is likely to do anything to you or your family. She hasn't made any reference to that at all.

Mrs. Smith: Well, I don't know. But I certainly hope you can do something. Thank you, Doctor. Goodbye.

SCENE V

Dr. Barry goes to talk with Mrs. Jones again. She again says she doesn't need to be in the hospital, and denies being angry at anyone. She concedes that the neighbors might have been a little worried about the gasoline, but needn't have been. She promises to fulfill her commitment to come to the clinic on Monday and assures the doctor that she'll be fine. . . . Dr. Barry returns to talk to Officer Peters.

Dr. Barry: I spoke with Mrs. Smith and then met with Mrs. Jones again, and I still don't think she should be admitted.

Officer Peters: *(Sighing)* Doc, what if she goes back home and goes at it again? What then? I mean, she's got problems. Anyone can see that . . .

Dr. Barry: I agree. But the law doesn't say you can hold somebody just because he or she has problems. Heaven knows, there are lots of times I've seen people like Mrs. Jones who need help, but according to the law in this state a person must be dangerous to himself or other persons beyond a reasonable doubt—and right now, I can't say that.

Officer Peters: Okay, Doc—but I sure hope she's like you say. I don't like taking her back home, but I guess there isn't anything else we can do now. We don't have any grounds to detain her at the station. You sure haven't been very much help to us tonight!

Point of View: Law Enforcement

In reviewing this vignette of a psychiatrist-police encounter, non-psychiatrists felt that the police officer showed elementary deficiencies. He had trouble gathering pertinent information and presenting it in a logical and coherent fashion; he failed to support the psychiatrist in his role; and ultimately he did not communicate efficiently or even courteously.

At the site of the disturbance, the officers were apparently influenced by the neighbors' remarks. Law enforcement professionals felt that the police officer was not trained to recognize the symptoms of possible mental disorders. Here again, the gathering of more complete information from the neighbors would have assisted in this process.

Distinction should have been made between Mrs. Jones's problem with alcohol and a psychotic condition, which would have helped to determine the appropriateness of an admission to a mental health facility. The necessity for treatment was viewed as a "way out" of the dilemma of the police officer who represents the interest of the community, as well as the individual. However, the officer should not have persisted in his judgments and generalities about Mrs. Jones's activities. These claims were neither challenged nor adequately explored by the psychiatrist. For example, Officer Peters stated that Mrs. Jones's house "was a shambles." "It looked like someone had gone absolutely berserk. She really did not seem to make too much sense."

In the second scene, Officer Peters may have overreacted. Mrs. Jones seemed to offer no serious threat to herself or to others, as she stated that her actions were misunderstood by her neighbors and the police officer.

In communicating with the doctor, the officers should have been more specific and detailed in their explanations of the patient's actions. Descriptive language such as "weirdo" or "bonkers" is neither helpful nor appropriate. While it is not mandatory that police officers use the technical jargon of the mental health professional, some common basis for discussion is necessary for effective communication.

The police officer offered the psychiatrist an interpretation of what the judge would find, namely, that "she did not belong in jail." A more thorough knowledge of the law by the officer might have avoided the commitment procedure and resulted in a consideration of an alternative placement because of Mrs. Jones's history of alcohol abuse. She could have been referred to an alcohol treatment facility or, with proper referral the next day, to another appropriate agency. In addition, if the officers had reassured the neighbors of the availability of other treatment agencies to deal with this problem, they would not have had the problem returned to them—a potentially dangerous situation.

In his attempt to convince the psychiatrist of the problem with Mrs. Jones, the officer did not clearly report the facts required to commit the individual, but instead interpreted the feelings of the community and the overall psychodynamics underlying the patient's actions. The officer's attempt to coerce the doctor (by telling him that the neighbors would be up in arms at Mrs. Jones's release) was judged to be inefficient, because it provoked the psychiatrist's resistance.

Finally, in such situations, police officers should not tell the doctor 'not to take too long because they have other calls they have to answer.' They should be encouraged to take whatever time is necessary to complete their work in this case. Trying to shift the problem onto someone else (since the officers had already arrived at a conclusion before arriving at the emergency room) did not encourage a cooperative spirit between the two agencies. The psychiatrist in turn should develop a clear understanding of, and respect for, the time pressures and shift difficulties in police work.

There were fewer criticisms of the psychiatrist's performance. Law enforcement reviewers felt that the psychiatrist did not fully explore the severity of the situation the officers observed when they arrived in the neighborhood. Such exploration might have precluded the reinforcement statements made by the police officer later, which lead to further opposition by the doctor.

Faced with Officer Peters' overreaction to the question of "serious threat," the psychiatrist could have explained Mrs. Jones's behavior and the rationale she offered. It was inappropriate for the physician to offer his interpretation of the law which was, "They have to be dangerous beyond a reasonable doubt." In such a situation, confrontation was much more likely since the officer may have had a different interpretation of the law. The doctor should avoid displaying a superior attitude, such as predicting what a judge would do in this kind of case.

The doctor's explanation of the patient's condition to the concerned neighbor was probably unnecessary. The psychiatrist did not challenge the neighbors' statements that the patient was "unpredictable" and "not stable." He might have been able to counteract some of the preconceived notions held by the neighbors.

While space availability is a real issue, it could have been addressed with the supervisor—keeping the patients' best interests foremost.

Point of View: Psychiatry

The psychiatrists reviewing this dialogue felt that the problem centered around: legal limitations of mental health commitment, poor communication between the psychiatrist and the police officer, as well as difficulties based on systems theory, role models, and power distribution.

Police officers have the obligation to protect citizens from harm by other persons. They look at behavior within environmental settings to predict when harm may be forthcoming. The psychiatrist, on the other hand, has a responsibility to evaluate the individual and keep him from harming himself or from harming others as a result of his mental illness. Knowing a person's behavior alone is not sufficient information for the psychiatrist who must examine motivation, intention, and dynamics.

A psychiatrist must acknowledge some limitations in treating alcoholics, particularly a person such as Mrs. Jones who has no meaningful source of psychological or social support. On the other hand, police officers are reluctant to charge a woman in such a predicament and know that the criminal justice system has little to offer her. Therefore, they turn to the psychiatrist for help in dealing with the neighbor's distress.

From the legal standpoint, although Mrs. Jones might have been helped in the short run by civil commitment, there was no evidence that long-term benefits could be derived, or that the patterns of behavior would have changed without the establishment of a definitive treatment program. The last statement notwithstanding, Dr. Barry's interpretation of the civil commitment process seems unnecessarily rigid. Dr. Barry appeared to be the one who was the strict constructionist. The setting of a fire close to the fence and the destruction of the furniture in her home could have been interpreted as dangerous behavior and Dr. Barry could have left the decision to release Mrs. Jones to the judge. Commitment could have allowed Mrs. Jones some time to "dry out," and efforts could have been made to involve her in a treatment program, return her to the VA, or get her involved, possibly in a group such as Alcoholics Anonymous. Obviously, as a side benefit, the police and the neighbors would also have been relieved.

Of special concern is to hear the psychiatrist taking a position which could be summarized as, "Well, if the law does not want us to interfere with people's rights, we will show them." In this circumstance he is avoiding clinical responsibilities and using the civil commitment law to justify his actions.

Using this concept, the role of the police officers is rather incidental. Repetition of such incidents would make the police officer seem ineffective because of his inability to deal with the disturbance. Police in large cities may have become hardened to situations like this long ago and it might be interesting to contrast the reaction of this officer to that of police in a more densely populated or urban area. The dialogue seemed to say more about the current preoccupation of psychiatry with commitment than about the difficulties with the law or the communication problems between the law enforcement and psychiatric professions. Civil commitment laws may change, but people like Mrs. Jones will still create problems in the community, and neighbors will continue to call the police until they learn that our institutional arrangements (the police, the criminal justice system, psychiatric hospitals) no longer offer any help.

By actions as are described in this dialogue, psychiatrists may be communicating that they either cannot or will not help law enforcement deal with the kind of situation Mrs. Jones presents. Law enforcement then may choose to educate the public that it must learn to live with the discomfort caused by people like Mrs. Jones or develop alternatives to involuntary psychiatric commitment. Alternatively, law enforcement may portray the problem to the public as a failure of psychiatry to respond to the seriously mentally ill.

Contact with a mental health professional or a law enforcement officer should be an educational experience for all involved. However, there seemed to be little teaching or learning in this case. Nor can there be unless the mental health professional is aware of possible conflicts or hidden agenda.

The "strict constructionist" interpretation should be left to the judge. This may represent a first step in educating judges that there is another way to look at human behavior and another way to interpret "dangerousness." A strict constructionist judge might attempt to interpret dangerousness in a "criminal law" manner rather than applying the more liberal definition generally utilized by mental health professionals. This concept of dangerousness as a criterion for commitment, when interpreted in a criminal justice manner, has caused much hardship to some patients who are unable to care for themselves outside of a hospital but who have been refused commitment. In this case, the doctor could have clarified for the judge his reasons for committing, whether or not the judge agrees. The police officer would then have been exposed to a form of reasoning similar to his own.

While the doctor should not completely accept the police officer's opinion as to the dangerousness of an individual, the officer's experience should be given some credence. He has constant contact with the public in many different situations, quite different from the experience of the average mental health professional. It appeared that the physician relied too much on his understanding of the law and/or his understanding of the judge's interpretation of the law. He should have been talking about the patient's behavior: the chances that this patient might get into greater difficulties, and the reason for believing this patient was not likely to commit any dangerous acts.

An additional problem in communication between these two people was reflected by the lack of alternatives presented to the officer should the patient get into further difficulty when returned home. This officer will have to deal with the woman and the reactions of her neighbors when she returns home. How can he deal with the neighbors' anxiety when he returns to the community?

A third area considered was the communication problem between psychiatrist and police officers.

The psychiatrist discussed violence and dangerous behavior. His communication to the police officer should include the potential for violent and/or dangerous behavior, even in people who are not mentally ill. It is this distinction between the mentally ill who may become violent as a result of their mental illness and those who may become violent because of other factors, such as excessive alcohol intake, frustration, or unresolved anger or hostility that must be communicated.

Communications here ought to stress a need for more appropriate management of this particular type of patient without jeopardizing her civil rights and also without jeopardizing the tranquility of her neighbors. An appropriate intermediate type of facility or treatment should be sought.

In this case it appears that the communications are not, in and of themselves, inadequate, but that they reflect the inadequacy of our societal institutions. Society has no formal mechanism to deal with these borderline cases, which are far more common than either the violent or the severely mentally ill.

These problems can be discussed further in the light of social role models. The officer exercised one role by taking Mrs. Jones into custody in an effort to "keep the peace" in the neighborhood, rather than shifting his role to the position of referring agent or of a petitioner on behalf of Mrs. Jones. He was disconcerted when the psychiatrist refused to carry out an expected role function (accepting a sick person for care). Additional disagreement, therefore, was generated.

The officer persisted in his peace-keeping and referring roles and tried to marshall forces to change the psychiatrist's position.

The psychiatrist, on the other hand, invoked language and thoughts familiar to the officer, raised the specter of the judge, and quoted the law as he attempted to explain the forces influencing him. Herein lies the major communication problem. Each participant brought to the confrontation burdens partially or largely uncomprehended by the other. To borrow a concept from group dynamics, each member came to the meeting as an agent of groups that he was expected to represent and lobby for. In the officer's case, it was the neighbors and his superior and, to some extent, Mrs. Jones. In the psychiatrist's case it was the statutes, the judge, and the hospital administration and, on a different level, the possibility of a malpractice suit.

Finally, the power issue: the psychiatrist won out because he was in a position of power. The officer, with Mrs. Jones in tow, was a visitor and petitioner to a social system alien to his own. He mobilized whatever power he had (the lieutenant and the neighbor), but was at a disadvantage from the beginning. Having determined that Mrs. Jones was not subject to arrest or legal detention and that she was ill, he could only plead for the neighbors and Mrs. Jones. The result of the confrontation was a stalemate. Mrs. Jones was returned to the community, having been found an unsuitable candidate for either the legal or psychiatric subsystem. One can hope that she did appear at the clinic on Monday. It is ironic that the two individuals in the confrontation wound up in nearly reversed role positions: the psychiatrist represented the law while the officer made a human service effort.

As a result of the difficulty with recent judicial and legislative constraints on psychiatric practice based upon interpretations of civil rights, the referral to appropriate community agencies has become an auxiliary police function. In spite of this trend, such referring functions seem to have received little attention in training programs.

Discussion

It is difficult to work within any system which has a complex technical pattern of communication when this system is partially controlled on different occasions by another system. When these two systems have a common area which may be viewed as belonging clearly to each side, then antagonism can arise.

The Police Officer

Police officers often hesitate when confronted with situations involving possible mental illness, particularly when major crimes are not involved. They feel inadequately equipped and are reminded by society, as well as by psychiatrists, that treating the sick as "hard core" criminals is inhumane. When the police officer responds by calling upon the psychiatrist for assistance and for relief from responsibility, the psychiatrist is often frustrated by the treatment difficulties which these patients present and angered by the limitations imposed by the law in dealing with other than the most obviously dangerous mentally ill person.

Frequently, when both parties disclaim responsibility for the person involved and blame each other, an intense confrontation arises, making communication and resolution difficult. Any solution requires these systems to develop an interface where more work can take place.

The first strategy involves definition of the boundary between law enforcement and mental health. In the case at hand, law enforcement and psychiatry should bring together a group of people dedicated to the resolution of boundary disputes. This may be achieved best by the appointment of experts to each group who are committed to participate in the resolution of problems which are perceived as outside the scope of the system's customary activities and responsibilities. A police department psychiatrist or psychologist who is available for consultation may become perceived as a mental health expert who is worthy of trust by both sides. His role would be to evaluate a situation and advise police officers. Because his authority stems from the police, the suspicion which usually develops in this situation can be decreased.

Similarly, if the psychiatric institution has access to a lawyer such as the county attorney or his/her deputies, its staff could gain credibility in any dialogue while, at the same time, be able to reduce their insecurity as they try to abide by laws which are difficult to interpret, often resented, and frequently perceived as leaving the doctor unprotected legally or ethically.

The boundary problem becomes most acute during times of crises, but cannot be resolved by the protagonists in an emergency room at midnight. Police officers and psychiatrists alike must recognize the constraints of the setting. Cooperation in the best interest of the patient and the involved agencies needs to prevail despite whatever disagreements over larger issues exist.

In spite of continuing confusion over boundaries, however, the collaboration in the emergency room can be constructive. The law enforcement agency can encourage the police officer to assist the doctor in the assessment process. The psychiatrist's assessment strategy in an emergency room should encompass a true understanding and evaluation of the patient's social network. It is not just the patient *in vacuo* who is being assessed, but his relationship to his environment. The police officer can often provide vital information.

The liberal use of supervisors, colleagues, or attorneys should be encouraged and should not be viewed by the psychiatrist as a defeat or sign of weakness. In obtaining second opinions and assistance, the psychiatrist will reinforce his credibility in the eyes of the police officer.

Late evening in the emergency room is not the time or place for the psychiatrist to lecture on the merits of the law, the judge's bias, or the unfortunate situation resulting from a scarcity of beds. When psychiatrists confront police officers in this way, the results will not be constructive. The officer faced with difficult legal constraints on his actions does not need any more hurdles in his path, particularly since he really has little to do with the makeup of a mental health law. The physician, therefore, needs to listen to the police officer and convey the message that he is not a barrier to their joint responsibility for the patient. The battle to convert each situation into either a "police case" or a "psychiatric case" is sterile and leads to an antagonism and defensiveness which reduces the chances for an effective resolution.

In some cases, temporary solutions can buy time to evaluate a difficult case. The ability to compromise will help achieve an appropriate disposition; thus, the placement of an uncertain case in jail or in the hospital setting for 12-24 hours can be appropriate if precautionary steps are taken to ensure medical, psychiatric and personal safety. Such compromises require the willingness of both parties to follow up the next day. The limitations of the evening/night situation can be overcome in most cases by the next day through further observation of the patient and through the utilization of resources not available during the crisis.

However, the framework for this "escape" mechanism must be developed in advance by both agencies. Professionals in law, psychiatry, and law enforcement should have a working alliance prior to the emergency room situation. Ventilation, discussion, and positive corrective planning will facilitate mutual understanding. As this understanding is communicated to those on the "front lines," the need to use stressful settings to accomplish hidden agenda items will be reduced.

The bottom line is that there is a set of laws which reduce the flexibility of both the police officer and psychiatrist. Both, in conjunction with society, will, therefore, have to develop alternatives to deal with those who are protected in their right to refuse treatment and who nevertheless must coexist in society. Forcing the community to accept them or forcing the police to handle them alone will only reinforce the isolation of the patient and lead to protraction and exacerbation of illness. Pressure is needed at the local level from both sides to raise the general population's awareness of this dilemma. We need to educate not only lawyers and police, but also politicians and the public.

Once the patient is in the hospital, the psychiatrist may encounter a different kind of conflict which illustrates another aspect of the interface between psychiatry and the law, namely communication with the patient advocate. This is illustrated in the vignette on the patient advocate.

3

**INTERFACE II
THE PATIENT ADVOCATE**

Acknowledgments

We gratefully acknowledge the assistance of the following in the preparation of this chapter:

Dean Brooks, *Superintendent, Oregon State Hospital, Salem OR*

Paul Friedman, *Director, Mental Health Law Project, Washington DC*

Milton Greenblatt, *Assistant Dean, School of Medicine; Professor and Vice Chairman, Department of Psychiatry and Behavioral Sciences; University of California Los Angeles, Los Angeles CA*

Robert E. Jones, *Clinical Professor of Psychiatry, Jefferson Medical College, Philadelphia PA*

Joel I. Klein, *Klein, Onek and Farr; General Counsel, American Psychiatric Association, Washington DC*

Laura M. LeWinn, *Deputy Director, Department of the Public Advocate, State of New Jersey, Trenton NJ*

Michael L. Perlin, *Director, Department of the Public Advocate, State of New Jersey, Trenton NJ*

Miles F. Shore, *Area Director and Superintendent, The Massachusetts Mental Health Center; Bullard Professor of Psychiatry, Harvard Medical School, Boston MA*

Robert Stolberg-Acosta, *Professor and Chairman, Department of Psychiatry, University of Puerto Rico, San Juan PR*

William J. Winslade, *Co-director, Program in Medicine, Law and Human Values; Lecturer, Law and Psychiatry, University of California at Los Angeles, Los Angeles CA*

3

Interface II

The Patient Advocate

DIALOGUE

SETTING: The following dialogue takes place in the nurses' station of a psychiatric ward in a teaching hospital in a large northwestern city.

PARTICIPANTS: Ms. Margaret Douglas: A lawyer
Dr. Thompson: A young psychiatrist
Thomas Dodge: (not present) a 16-year-old boy hospitalized for severe behavioral problems including fighting and fire-setting
Mr. Dodge: Thomas's long-suffering father
Mrs. Constance Smith: A psychiatric nurse

Ms. Douglas: Dr. Thompson, Mr. Dodge (*shaking hands*), I'm glad I could meet with you both to discuss a hearing for Thomas.

Mr. Dodge: A hearing? What's he done this time? What's this about? I just got a call to meet a lawyer today. Has Tom managed to get himself in trouble inside the hospital?

Ms. Douglas: No, no, don't worry, Mr. Dodge. Your son isn't in any kind of trouble. I work for the Mental Health Information Service. I'm employed by the state to represent hospitalized psychiatric patients in any grievances they have against the hospital. Thomas is questioning some aspects of his treatment, as well as the hospitalization itself, which is against his will. It's my job in this situation to advise and represent Thomas at the hearing. As Dr. Thompson is aware, we often try to mediate cases like this to avoid a hearing, but after speaking with Thomas, I believe he is quite determined to go to court, and he seems to have some valid complaints.

Mr. Dodge: Wait a minute. I don't believe this. Of course he's in the hospital against his will. The kid was acting like a lunatic. We couldn't handle him at home, and I signed him into the hospital. He needs help. Isn't it up to me and his doctor to decide when he's ready to leave?

Ms. Douglas: Usually, yes. A patient is discharged when the patient, his family and doctor agree that he's ready. But at any time, any patient, regardless of age, can have a hearing before a judge, at which the burden of proof falls on the hospital to establish the need for further hospitalization. If the judge decides in favor of the hospital, your son will stay here. If the judge decides in favor of your son, he will be free to leave the hospital. Of course, we like to take into consideration the family's feelings in a situation like this.

Mr. Dodge: Now I'm really confused! What was the point of my going to all that effort to get him into the hospital if he can get out whenever he wants? Besides, he's only sixteen. He's still a minor. I thought I had legal control over him until he was eighteen. That's what they explained to us when I signed him in here.

Ms. Douglas: Yes, it's a bit complicated. Legally, you do have control over your children until their eighteenth birthday, including committing them to a psychiatric hospital against their will. I should add that, although this is currently the law, a number of cases are pending that could reverse it. However, once your child is admitted to a psychiatric facility, he has the right to contest the hospitalization and, of course, the right to legal counsel in doing so. A parent cannot waive his child's legal rights in this instance.

Mr. Dodge: Where the hell does that leave me? The doctor tells me I can sign him in; you tell me he can sign himself out.

Ms. Douglas: It's probably something that will have to be decided in court. It's not just up to your son, remember. He'll have to convince a judge. As I said, we usually try to mediate these situations out of court, and I had hopes of doing that when I came here today.

Dr. Thompson: I wonder if we can't discuss this further with Thomas. I certainly wouldn't want to go to court if we could possibly avoid it. You mentioned that Thomas is contesting some aspects of his treatment?

Ms. Douglas: One aspect of his treatment that Thomas has mentioned is the daily community meetings. He claims that personal information about him is divulged at these meetings, and there is constant pressure for him to discuss personal and family matters.

Mr. Dodge: Well, I'd go along with that. I don't want our family affairs discussed with strangers. Doctor, I thought you said everything was confidential. We've told you a lot about our family. You know, I'd like to see just what information you have about Thomas and our family. I'd like to see his chart. I don't even know what his diagnosis is!

Dr. Thompson: I think I've discussed Tom's condition with you quite openly. There's nothing we're hiding from you about your son. It is a hospital policy that access to the charts is restricted to the hospital staff taking care of your son.

Mr. Dodge: And that includes, I suppose, the ladies' auxiliary and the guy who mops the floors.

Ms. Douglas: If it makes you feel better, as your son's lawyer, I have access to his records and can advise him about his rights in respect to privacy.

Mr. Dodge: No. that doesn't make me feel any better. You know, I'm not so worried about my son—he seems to have plenty of rights. Maybe I need to see a lawyer to see what rights I have. I'm the one who ends up having to take care of my son when you folks are through. (*Walks off angrily*)

Dr. Thompson: It's a shame he's so upset. I think having his son hospitalized has been quite a strain on him.

Ms. Douglas: I'm sorry he left, too. This matter will be more complicated if Thomas's father is opposed to what he wants. Another thing Thomas complained about was getting medication against his will. From reading his original treatment plan, it didn't appear that he was going to get medication.

Dr. Thompson: He doesn't really—maybe something now and then when he is disturbed. Wait, here's the head nurse, Mrs. Smith. I'll ask her. Mrs. Smith, about how often has Thomas Dodge received medication since he's been here?

Mrs. Smith: Not often enough, if you ask me. The staff has meant to talk to you about that. The resident won't order anything except when he's wild, but that kid needs medication. Last week one of our aides got attacked by a patient over on 4 South and the staff is pretty nervous about this Thomas Dodge. He's quite provocative to the other patients as well as the staff, and I'm afraid someone's going to get hurt.

Dr. Thompson: I should have introduced you, Mrs. Smith. This is Ms. Douglas, the mental health lawyer representing Thomas. Thomas has complained about receiving medication, and we really won't be able to change his medication until we've gone to the hearing.

Mrs. Smith: I understand that, but I'm worried that there will be a lot of staff calling in sick within the next week, unless we're able to medicate these patients adequately. The situation just gets out of hand sometimes and we have our rights, too. (*Walks away abruptly*)

Dr. Thompson: One more problem. (*Shaking his head*) Getting back to this hearing business, though, it really would be a shame to have to go to court. I certainly support legal rights for patients and there have been abuses in the past, but don't you agree, there are just some built-in contradictions to this process. The law is really based on 18th century philosophical assumptions about human nature and how people behave. We've learned a lot since then. The law assumes that every person is capable of recognizing and operating in his own best interest. If that were true, there wouldn't be any need for psychiatric hospitals.

Ms. Douglas: But it's always been the medical profession that has wanted to define other people's limitations for them. People don't trust doctors to decide who is sick and who is well any more. Overall, I think it works out better if we leave it up to individuals to decide if they want to be helped or if they feel sick, rather than giving that power to a professional or an agency.

Dr. Thompson: Isn't that hypocritical? It seems to me that a lot of this rights business just means that lawyers and judges will be deciding for people instead of doctors.

Ms. Douglas: But in the legal system the patient has

representation to defend his own interests, rather than be subject to the opinion of one doctor.

Dr. Thompson: I wonder about all this. I don't think Mr. Dodge felt too protected today. We have to deal with the effects of all this on both the patient and the family, too. Take this case for instance. We're pretending that the effect of the legal process is neutral, but it's not. To go through this process could be therapeutically damaging to a boy like Tommy. He's never had any sensible limits set for him, and he's terrified of his own aggression. He's become a master at manipulating the adults in his environment so they end up fighting with each other about him, and no one is left to be the responsible adult he needs. The first priority in any treatment for him is to give him that consistent environment he needs. Instead, we're acting out the same pattern that he's always created in his environment and this won't do him any good.

Ms. Douglas: That sounds fine on paper, but you're overlooking one thing. The patient says he doesn't want this kind of help and however well-meaning your efforts are, I think his rejection of help somewhat invalidates your theories. And in the meanwhile, the patient is being restricted and coerced in concrete, tangible ways.

Dr. Thompson: I hate to say this, but you're letting yourself be manipulated by him. He's always set himself up as the victim and attracted the aggression of others toward him. That's a major part of his pathology as well as a desperate attempt to establish some boundaries for his aggression and guilt.

Ms. Douglas: It's a little frightening to think of what could be justified with reasoning like that. You've transformed the patient's saying he wants to leave the hospital into a plea to stay in the hospital. That kind of psychiatric "double-think" is exactly why mental patients need representation.

Dr. Thompson: You're talking about abstract cases. We have to deal with real lives. Do you ever think about what the consequences of a hearing will be on a patient? I fear most for Thomas if he "wins" his hearing. Not only will he lose the opportunity for treatment, but he can only become more terrified and guilty about his own aggression. If he's released through a court order, I wouldn't be surprised if he has to "up the ante," so to speak, and engage in real criminal activities. In fact, I wouldn't rule out the possibility of self-destructive behavior.

Ms. Douglas: I'm afraid your attempt at psychological blackmail won't work. Nor will your blaming the legal system for your failures to adequately treat patients. I think we should discuss this further in court, Dr. Thompson. Good-bye.

Point of View: Patient Advocate

The reaction of lawyers to this deliberately over-dramatized dialogue is very similar to that of psychiatrists. The same points are made although with some difference in emphasis and in attitudes toward them. While doctors as well as lawyers talk about the rights of their patients, and lawyers, like the doctors, talk about appropriate treatment, both are concerned with putting a hearing to "constructive therapeutic use." Lawyers even borrow the language of dynamic psychiatry to caution physicians against "the employment of such defenses as denial and resistance" in dealing with the reality of the legal system.

Lawyers, likewise, call attention to the differences in outlook between themselves and psychiatrists. For them, the paramount value is not health, but liberty, which is seen as a precondition to health and happiness. They see Dr. Thompson, at best, as a well-meaning person who, because of zeal rather than malice, is likely to encroach on Thomas's liberty. At worst, they question Dr. Thompson's motives and those of the patient's father. ("... many children are victimized by their families ... a family's pathology is often attributed to the child, who is then exiled to an institution.")

Lawyers see themselves as being process-oriented rather than person-oriented and emphasize the need for rules and procedures.

Most of all, they see Dr. Thompson and mental health professionals in general as defending a social role, as "protecting turf." They believe that psychiatry resents the encroachment of another profession, such as law, into the treatment of the mentally ill.

They see a hearing for Thomas as a good thing, one that will satisfy his sense of fairness and need to be heard. It is suggested that the judge can arrange proper treatment for the patient and family, treatment not limited to the alternatives of institutionalization or return to a hostile, frustrated family. The judge can order a thorough review of existing community alternatives and may even mandate the creation of an appropriate community placement.

Lawyers comment on the futility of Dr. Thompson's trying to persuade Ms. Douglas to his way of thinking ("She did not choose her job because she was inclined to agree with Dr. Thompson's views"). Even if Ms. Douglas could be convinced, another lawyer who disagrees is bound to come along. Had Dr. Thompson seen Ms. Douglas privately and not antagonized her or engaged in a "philosophical" discussion, he might have achieved some modest goals. He could have found out her grievances and worked with her to make some changes that would satisfy her concerns (and those of her client?).

Knowing the emphasis lawyers place on rationality, liberty and process, one is not surprised to find Ms. Douglas saying that speculation cannot be used as a basis on which to deny the patient procedural due process. This, in spite of Dr. Thompson's concern that the hearing might cause the patient guilt feelings.

However, lawyers do note that the first obligation of both professions is to the patient/client, and therein lies the possibility of collaboration rather than conflict.

Point of View: Psychiatry

The psychiatrist begins by wondering why this conversation took place, as it did, in the nurses' station rather than in an office or conference room where the patient's privacy would have been better protected and interruptions, such as that by the nurse, Mrs. Smith, would have been less likely to occur.

It is suggested that Dr. Thompson erred by trying to discuss the problem for the first time with the lawyer while the patient's father was present. Had he been able to give full attention to the attorney he might have been able to make better use of her apparent willingness to at least consider mediation.

Likewise, in talking initially to the father on a one-to-one basis he might have given the father more help in understanding the possible need for a hearing and dealt more effectively with the father's very real concerns. Dr. Thompson does not clarify hospital policy concerning confidentiality, nor does he explain the nature and value of group therapy. He does not acknowledge the father's concern about his rights as a parent, nor does he direct the father to a source of help or legal advice about those rights.

Indeed, Dr. Thompson, caught up in the legal issue, seems to overlook the emotional needs of the patient's family, just as, at times, he seems to lose sight of his primary obligation to help the patient.

After the initial discussion it might have been desirable to involve the patient in a meeting with the lawyer, appropriate staff members, and family members to see if the problems could be resolved without the need for a hearing. Dr. Thompson suggests, "I wonder if we can't discuss this further with Thomas," but he fails to pursue this altogether reasonable option.

It would appear that before talking to anyone, Dr. Thompson should have reviewed the case more carefully and at least have known what medication had been given, when, and why. The implication that medication was being used to control behavior for the convenience of hospital employees ("administrative sedation") rather than to benefit the patient is unfortunate, if it was untrue. If true, the patient did need an attorney to protect his rights.

Psychiatrist readers suggested improvement in almost every one of Dr. Thompson's comments. Probably Dr. Thompson could, too, as he reflected on this discussion. Ms. Douglas would very likely have been, at best, an adversary, since our legal system is after all an adversary system. However, Dr. Thompson could have sought a common ground for compromise by focusing on a search for ways of meeting Thomas's needs while protecting his rights, and avoid antagonizing his adversary. Dr. Thompson could have been less defensive and done a better job of dealing with the reality of the situation.

In addition to a general critique of Dr. Thompson's handling of the interview, psychiatrist readers highlight two points which are problems for them in dealing with the legal system.

One major difference in the outlook of lawyers from that of psychiatrists is the lack of understanding (or acceptance) of unconscious determinants of behavior. The lawyer sees not only the average person but the mentally ill person as well as being rational, in possession of free will, and capable of making decisions in her or his own best interest. The lawyer tends to take statements at face value and to believe that a patient's demand, for example, is straightforward evidence of what he or she really wants. The psychiatrist sees this as incredibly naive. However, when the psychiatrist attempts to communicate some understanding of unconscious factors influencing behavior, he tends to use technical jargon. Use of jargon the lawyer does not understand causes her to reject the formulations as convoluted, meaningless psychologizing. Likewise, if the psychiatrist suggests that the patient cannot make decisions in his or her own best interests, the lawyer feels that the psychiatrist is arrogant and is accusing anyone who does not agree with his clinical recommendation of being crazy.

In addition, psychiatrists have a concern, even a feeling of guilt, about a group of patients who can no longer be treated. These guilt feelings are evoked when such a patient is encountered. The voluntary patient can accept a need for help and seek it out, give informed consent for appropriate treatment, or get a second opinion if in doubt, and the "mentally ill dangerous person" can be treated as an involuntary patient. But there are a number of other patients whose needs are not being met.

One psychiatrist reader commented about this group: "We want the legal profession to understand that there exists a group of mentally ill people whose illnesses deprive them of the knowledge that they need care and can benefit from proper care, and that we psychiatrists want to cooperate with lawyers and legislators to find legal ways, respecting the rights of man, by which we all can help these neglected sick."

Discussion

No reader among the psychiatrists or lawyers ventured the suggestion that Dr. Thompson should have had advice of counsel before and during his encounter with Ms. Douglas. Likewise, no one suggested that he might have avoided the encounter altogether by having her talk with his attorney, or having her talk with the hospital administrator. Both of these options are worthy of consideration.

The legal system is an adversary system and opposing attorneys take the roles of gladiators, or at least debaters, with years of training for this type of combat. The non-attorney attempting to deal single-handedly with such a gladiator is probably the sort of person who would volunteer to spar a few rounds with Muhammad Ali.

The adversary system is uncomfortable for the psychiatrist who does not, of course, see himself as an adversary of the patient. Rather, he finds that role incompatible with therapeutic collaboration. The administrator, though also perceiving himself as a helping person, can more easily take sides. The administrator can side against the patient, or at least against the patient's desire to leave a hospital prematurely, to refuse needed medication, or whatever. Involvement of others, which leaves the treating physician out of the legal hassle, can help keep that physician from being cast in an anti-therapeutic role.

However, if the psychiatrist must deal with the attorney, several recommendations can be derived from the comments of psychiatrists and lawyers:

- The psychiatrist should accept the fact that the legal profession's involvement in mental health care is a reality that won't go away.

- The physician needs to understand, and accept as legitimate, the values and biases of the legal profession.

- In a situation of the sort illustrated by the dialogue, the psychiatrist should recognize the futility of trying to convert the lawyer to a psychiatric point of view, and should try to avoid being defensive, antagonistic, or argumentative.

- The psychiatrist should identify the attorney's concerns and seek compromises that will still allow effective treatment of the patient.

- Mental health professionals cannot expect to have their professional opinion about a patient's competence accepted without challenge. In order to establish that the patient is not competent, the psychiatrist should avoid technical psychiatric explanations. Instead, he should use illustrations from actual behavior that will make the point as clear as possible to non-psychiatrists who may believe that psychiatric theory is hogwash.

- Speculations or predictions on what may happen are futile. If one can offer statistics they may help, but past actions and their consequences are more likely to be convincing.

- In the words of one of the attorneys: "If all else fails, I guess Dr. Thompson should go to court and help some judge understand why Mr. Dodge's son needs to be hospitalized. It may seem like a silly system, but in some states it is the only one we have that will allow children to remain hospitalized."

While the patient is in the hospital, the psychiatrist may also have to plead the patient's cause to the representative of the third-party payor, as in Interface III.

4

**INTERFACE III
THE THIRD-PARTY PAYOR**

Acknowledgments

We gratefully acknowledge the assistance of the following in the preparation of this chapter:

Paul Chodoff, *Clinical Professor of Psychiatry, George Washington University, Washington DC*

William Guillette, *Medical Director, Aetna Life and Casualty, Hartford CT*

Walter J. McNerney, *President, Blue Cross Association, Chicago IL*

Robert A. Nover, *Chief, Clinical Infant Research Section, Mental Health Study Center, Division of Mental Health Service Programs, National Institute of Mental Health, Adelphi MD*

Norman R. Penner, *Director, APA-CHAMPUS Peer Review Project, Washington DC*

Alexander Richman, *Department of Psychiatry and Preventive Medicine, Dalhousie University, Halifax, Nova Scotia, Canada*

Steven S. Sharfstein, *Special Assistant to the Director, National Institute of Mental Health, Rockville MD*

4

Interface III

The Third-Party Payor

DIALOGUE

SETTING: Some of the issues and controversy involved in third-party payment for psychiatric illness are illustrated in the following vignette. The setting is the office of the Medical Director of "Continental Mutual Insurance Company."

PARTICIPANTS: Fred Smith, M.D., Medical Director, Continental Mutual Insurance Company
Donald Johnson, M.D., Medical Director, Pinecrest Hospital, a private nonprofit psychiatric hospital with a large adolescent treatment unit

This is one of a series of meetings between these two doctors over insurance coverage for adolescents.

Dr. Johnson: Good morning, Dr. Smith. Happy to see you again. I came to discuss the case of Jane Williams. Have you seen the chart?

Dr. Smith: Yes, what seems to be the problem with the case?

Dr. Johnson: This 16-year-old girl was hospitalized at Pinecrest for nearly four months earlier this year. Your office denied payment of benefits for the last six weeks of her stay, claiming that hospitalization was no longer medically necessary and the diagnosis did not warrant such a long stay. We feel very strongly that you're mistaken in this decision and that you have no basis for refusing to pay for the full hospitalization.

Dr. Smith: We certainly need to discuss this case further, since it's typical of the problem we have with psychiatric claims. First, let's look at the question of the diagnosis. This girl was admitted with two diagnoses; the first was an acute toxic psychosis due to cocaine, and the second was an adjustment reaction of adolescence. Which one was responsible for the admission?

Dr. Johnson: Well, the drug psychosis was actually responsible for the admission, but it was part of a larger picture. The girl had been abusing a number of drugs, especially stimulants, for over a year. In addition, she had demonstrated a general deterioration in behavior, social life, emotional stability and intellectual functioning. She was often truant from school, was always fighting with her parents, was acting out sexually, and had begun selling drugs in order to pay for her own habit. On the day of admission, she had been using cocaine heavily when she suddenly became frightened, upset, and very paranoid. She accused her mother of "bugging" her room, started fighting with her and, during the fight, pushed her mother down some stairs. The police were called and charged the girl with assault, and she was then admitted to a closed unit at Pinecrest under a court commitment.

Dr. Smith: So the drug psychosis was the reason for her hospitalization?

Dr. Johnson: The immediate reason, yes. But it was only part of the whole picture of a long-standing personality problem and serious drug abuse. The psychosis was only the tip of the iceberg.

Dr. Smith: Well, how long did the drug psychosis take to clear?

Dr. Johnson: She was no longer psychotic after a week, but she remained very depressed, angry and resistant for another few weeks. She remained on a closed unit for over five weeks before she could be trusted on an open unit.

Dr. Smith: Do you mean that you kept her on a closed unit because she was upset about staying in the hospital and would have run away if she had a chance?

Dr. Johnson: It's not that simple. Such depression and anger are often seen in stimulant drug users when they withdraw from the drugs. She certainly didn't want to stay in the hospital; she wanted to see certain friends who would have supplied her with drugs. For these reasons, we needed to confine her on a locked unit. Since she was committed, we were legally obliged to keep her and to treat her in a secure setting.

Dr. Smith: How do you know that her anger and unhappiness weren't due to the confinement itself? Maybe she was upset because she was committed, rather than vice-versa. I sometimes think that your young patients act crazier when they're locked up than if they weren't confined. But, in any event, it's clear that her hospitalization after recovery from the drug psychosis was mainly for the purpose of controlling her desire for drugs and preventing her escape from the hospital. Couldn't that have been done somewhere else, such as a juvenile shelter or residential drug program?

Dr. Johnson: But there are no therapeutic or diagnostic services available in such places. Besides, that view ignores the fact that confinement may be an essential part of therapy by protecting a patient from his impulses, especially when the impulses are self-destructive. Kids like this don't handle freedom very well; confinement doesn't create disturbed behavior, but only brings it into sharper focus. The adolescent with a severe personality problem may avoid confronting his illness until he is confined for a long period and cut off from his usual methods of relieving tension and seeking gratification. Kids like this often cannot be treated outside a hospital because on the outside, they use their antisocial behavior or drug abuse to avoid issues in therapy.

Dr. Smith: Perhaps so. But let me get back to the problem of the diagnosis. After about six weeks, the primary diagnosis was changed to schizophrenia, latent type. Why was the change made; isn't the second one a more serious diagnosis?

Dr. Johnson: Well, after recovering from the psychotic state, and after the anger and the craving had subsided, Jane remained fairly depressed and impulsive in her behavior. It was evident that the underlying problem was not an adjustment reaction. It was not situationally related and did not simply result from prolonged drug abuse. It became apparent that she had a borderline personality, a permanent type of personality organization which is not obviously psychotic but which shares some traits with the psychotic and some with the neurotic person. Some people have said that this personality is on the border of schizophrenia, so we usually place such a patient in the latent schizophrenic category.

Dr. Smith: What is the average length of hospitalization for full-blown schizophrenics at your hospital?

Dr. Johnson: Well, the average schizophrenic, if there is such a person, stays an average of 38 days; but some, especially the paranoid, may average somewhat longer.

Dr. Smith: Then why would someone who is not a full-blown schizophrenic stay nearly 120 days? And why was the diagnosis not made until she was already in the hospital for more than 40 days?

Dr. Johnson: The borderline patient is in many ways harder to treat than one that is severely psychotic. Medication may return a psychotic patient to reality and sometimes even to normal functioning in just a few weeks, while the borderline patient was never normal in the first place and requires a great deal of intensive psychotherapy in order to begin progress toward a normal personality development.

Dr. Smith: So therapy is needed to help them grow up, to complete the job the family didn't do right. That doesn't sound like an illness to me, and certainly seems different from the types of schizophrenia I learned about in medical school.

Dr. Johnson: It certainly is different from the usual types of schizophrenia you learned about. And yet, the borderline patient can become very depressed, even suicidal, and can act just as bizarre as a full-blown schizophrenic. We are also concerned about preventing the deterioration of these adolescents into a frank psychosis when they get older. We feel that early intervention may help prevent a lifelong downhill course, and may also prevent the further deterioration of the family situation. In this case, the mother was very upset over the patient's behavior and also was under treatment for depression. The daughter had driven a wedge between mother and father, and Mr. Williams was on the brink of leaving the family because of their disagreements about Jane.

Dr. Smith: Wait a minute! You know very well that Continental Mutual doesn't pay for preventive medical services, not for the patient and certainly not for a family member who is not even a patient. Besides, do you have any statistics to show how many of these borderline schizophrenics go on to develop regular schizophrenia?

Dr. Johnson: No, I don't really have any figures. But we do know that without treatment, they can become more seriously disturbed with time, maybe drink or use drugs heavily, and get in trouble with the law. With regard to the question of prevention, it's really shortsighted not to treat the patient early in life so as to reduce insurance payments later on. As for the family, unless we treat the families, our young patients will return to the same pressures which may have led to their illness in the first place.

Dr. Smith: Well now, who is the patient? Is the family borderline also? What's their diagnosis? To go back to the question of diagnosis, it looks as though you had a kid who couldn't get along with her family, became hooked on drugs, and flipped out while high on cocaine. That was your diagnosis of her until she was in the hospital for so long that you couldn't justify it unless you gave her a diagnosis of some major illness. Then, out comes this borderline schizophrenia, which sounds serious enough but then it turns out not really to be schizophrenia.

Dr. Johnson: There were several problems present which are typical in the treatment of adolescents. First, the family is often in as much need of treatment as the patient. This particular family *was* borderline in function and unless the mother's depression is also treated, the patient has little chance of successfully returning home. As for the question of diagnosis, we try to avoid labeling patients as psychotic whenever possible, so we often use the adjustment reaction diagnosis in cases where any doubt exists. We use the schizophrenic label carefully and this may explain why there was a delay in changing to the final diagnosis. Although this borderline state doesn't present the same symptoms as traditional schizophrenia, it's the only way we can understand the shifting moods, the self-destructive behavior, the disturbed interpersonal relations, the poor self-concept, and the immaturity of the personality. Although they may not be actively psychotic at any given time, they can regress under pressure and be quite disturbed, as this patient was on several occasions. Many psychiatrists feel that treating this kind of personality in adolescence can prevent the development of much more serious problems in adult life.

Dr. Smith: Well, I've never seen much convincing evidence about the value of prevention in psychiatry. But in any event, what you describe of the family suggests that maybe the only reason for the patient's long hospital stay is that the family wasn't able to take her back home. If that's true, the extended hospitalization was mainly for social reasons, not medical. That's our basic reason for denying coverage during the last six weeks. We can't pay for hospitalization if the patient could just as well have gone to a boarding school with some outpatient psychiatric treatment. Couldn't that have been done instead of keeping her in the hospital so long?

Dr. Johnson: We did consider placing her in the Davis school, which would have provided the therapy in a residential school setting. However, schools like this cost $15,000-$20,000 per year and aren't covered by insurance. The family couldn't afford this expense so we were forced to treat the patient until she was able to return home and then have outpatient therapy.

Dr. Smith: I was right. A less restrictive and less expensive alternative was available, and you did keep her hospitalized longer than needed.

Dr. Johnson: That's not quite true. The family couldn't afford the school alternative, and the State Division of Youth and Family Services is no longer paying for out-of-state placement for adolescents.

Dr. Smith: That's not the fault of Continental Mutual; we're in the health insurance business, not private schools. We can't pay for care which is not medically necessary, and you haven't shown that the final part of this patient's hospitalization was medically justified. To me, it's the same situation as the geriatric patient who could be cared for in a nursing home but remains in the hospital for social reasons.

Dr. Johnson: But a recent court decision in the Monmouth Medical Center case clearly stated that a hospital must be reimbursed for care given to a patient if no nursing home beds could be found. I think that this is a similar situation.

Dr. Smith: Except that we still don't have to pay for care given a patient who remains hospitalized only because the family can't take him home. I don't see why we should pay to keep this girl in the hospital until the family gets straightened out and can take her. I've looked at the nursing notes on her chart, which describe her as calm, cheerful, cooperative and involved in activities during her last six weeks in the hospital. It sounds like any other 16-year-old girl, not one who needed to be in the hospital.

Dr. Johnson: She certainly was improved, but at that time she was involved in active psychotherapy. She was in daily group therapy, family therapy once a week, and individual therapy three or four times a week. That's not custodial care and she clearly needed that intensity of psychotherapy before she was able to function back at home, at school, and with her old friends. You certainly must admit that she was receiving active treatment during that time. The nursing notes only describe her superficial level of behavior, not her level of treatment. Furthermore, there is often no correspondence between the behavior described by a nurse and the seriousness of an illness or the need for treatment.

Dr. Smith: Again, I must repeat that we are not paying for diagnosis or frequency of therapy, but only for medical necessity for hospitalization. I'm sure our society has lots of so-called borderline patients walking around who are in need of intensive therapy but who are functioning well on a superficial basis. Besides, couldn't this patient have been treated in a partial hospitalization program which could have provided the therapy, gotten her out of the home most of the day, and cost much less money?

Dr. Johnson: Except that insurance doesn't cover partial hospitalization programs, and the family couldn't afford the $60 or $70 a day required to deliver such intensive therapy in a partial hospitalization program.

Dr. Smith: You're mistaken if you think Continental Mutual should pay for expensive hospital care just because the family can't afford the more appropriate and less expensive alternatives.

Dr. Johnson: But the family purchased insurance to provide medical care when needed. If the insurance industry provided a broad spectrum of coverage for day care and outpatient treatment, perhaps some of these patients wouldn't be hospitalized for so long.

Dr. Smith: But I suspect that if we provided the broader outpatient and day care services you suggest, we would see these overutilized just as the inpatient services are. We can establish some hard criteria for medical necessity of inpatient care so that we can try to prevent abuses by hospitals, but it's almost impossible to determine the medical necessity of outpatient psychiatric treatment. I'm afraid we just can't depend on psychiatrists to make realistic determinations of medical necessity for outpatients, and it would be very hard to prevent abuses of outpatient benefits. You psychiatrists don't even agree among yourselves as to who requires outpatient psychotherapy, and how much any particular patient needs. It seems that there's a general principle operating in psychiatric treatment by which the medically necessary utilization expands to fill the available benefits. I wonder if that principle explains why your patient's hospitalization just happened to be for almost four months?

Dr. Johnson: What do you mean?

Dr. Smith: The patient's policy allows for 120 days of full hospital benefits, after which a 50 percent co-payment is required. You discharged the patient just five days before she entered the co-payment period, which suggests that the length of hospitalization was determined more by the extent of her benefits than by her actual level of improvement.

Dr. Johnson: Well, it may be that her date of discharge was influenced by the length of full coverage since the family couldn't have afforded an extended period of hospitalization at a 50 percent co-payment. But, after all, her policy did extend coverage for that period of 120 days.

Dr. Smith: That's just why we have problems with so many claims for psychiatric treatment. The patient's policy only covers hospital treatment for medical necessity; the policy is not an invitation to stay in the hospital for as long as possible up to the limit of coverage regardless of necessity.

Dr. Johnson: Maybe that's because most insurance policies don't provide coverage for a period adequate for many of the more serious psychiatric conditions. We see many patients with only 30 days of psychiatric coverage who are discharged prematurely because their coverage expires.

Dr. Smith: But I suspect that if we increased the coverage, the length of stay in these same cases would increase to equal the longer period of coverage. That kind of practice subverts the purpose of health insurance, which is to provide protection against the expenses of illness, not to provide rehabilitation, education or social services.

Dr. Johnson: I don't know how you can make such a clear distinction between active medical treatment and rehabilitation in psychiatric therapy. Social services can be essential in preventing a relapse of a psychotic state, and it may be impossible to treat a serious psychiatric illness without also providing some social and rehabilitative services. An example is the statement in your claims denial that the regular weekend visits home for the last three weeks prove that hospitalization was not necessary. Unless we were able to observe the family's interaction and the patient's behavior with them, we really couldn't have evaluated the medical necessity for her staying at the hospital. The illness we were treating was manifested by social conflict, so we had to use some social situations to measure the medical condition.

Dr. Smith: Well, in our opinion, when a patient starts going home every weekend she's no longer a hospital patient, but is in a boarding school. At that point, there are probably a number of other less costly places she could have gone to if going home wasn't possible.

Dr. Johnson: If society offered a range of facilities for improving patients, we might be able to move them out of the hospital sooner. There was nothing accessible to the patient and family between hospital and home, so the necessary treatment needed to be carried out in the hospital. To send her home prematurely might have led to another admission later on, for either the patient or perhaps her mother. Unless you in the insurance business see that sick adolescents must be treated in the context of their families and society, these kids will cause trouble again and again, and cost all of us more than just money.

Point of View: Third-Party Payor

In the foregoing dialogue, both sides believe in the rightness of their course. Each party is motivated by certain organizational or individual needs which range from protecting his job to safeguarding the financial security of the organization. Unfortunately, the protagonists in this dialogue see only the legitimacy of their own position and make little or no effort to recognize the existence of the needs of the other.

Certain assumptions can be made about Dr. Johnson. He seems to be an ethical, competent psychiatrist who has done his professional best to treat his patient's illness. He did what he felt was in the best interests of his patient, and thus, felt justified in being upset over the denial of payment by the insurance company. He perceived that denial as questioning his professional judgment and competence, and it obviously affects the cash flow at his institution.

Dr. Smith, meanwhile, is obviously a loyal employee of the insurance company who knows the importance of making responsible decisions as a guardian of the company's resources. He knows the stipulated coverage of the insurance contract, and attempted to be as precise as he could in defining medical necessity and appropriate hospitalization up to 120 days. One can assume that this case is not the only one which he must resolve in the course of a routine day, and he is, no doubt, aware that his decision had some impact on the patient, her family, and on Dr. Johnson, as well as on the insurance company. If he is injudicious in making decisions and permits payments in excess of premium income, he can prompt an increase in premium rates, dissatisfied beneficiaries, people defecting to other insurance plans, and a diminished competitive position for his company with regard to the health insurance industry.

It is also safe to assume that Dr. Smith is not a psychiatrist and, therefore, he brings with him certain doubts, perceptions and biases toward psychiatry which are held in common by many non-psychiatrist physicians. He does not see the hospital as a place to confine juveniles in order to protect them from a harmful environment, nor does he see prevention as a treatment goal in the same way a psychiatrist might. He has a narrow view of the medical responsibility which may be appropriate when discussing surgery for breast cancer or medical treatment of a peptic ulcer. He is aware of many of the weaknesses of psychiatry—disagreement among the psychiatric profession concerning appropriate therapies, poor outcome studies and inadequate statistics. Further, he is aware of the tendency of psychiatric services to be sustained for as long as the insurance coverage allows, implying that such services would expand if coverage were increased.

The impasse reflects some underlying real differences about what constitutes illness and treatment. Ultimately, the resolution of that impasse will depend on what the larger society decides about what conditions and what kinds of treatment it is willing to pay for under the aegis of health insurance.

In the case discussion between Drs. Johnson and Smith, there was little reference to the contents of the medical record. The psychiatrist referred to nursing notes and diagnosis, but not to clinical formulation, treatment plan or progress notes. The insurance company reviewer repeatedly had to infer clinical considerations without support from clinical record. For the third-party payor to effectively assess the need for treatment, the medical record must show the documentation of the successive shifts in clinical concerns, therapeutic goals and clinical status. In the absence of such documentation, it is difficult for the third-party payor to identify medical necessity.

In addition, it is important for the patient's psychiatrist and clinical supervisors to be informed of third-party payor concerns. They should be oriented to the meaning of "medical necessity," "level of care," and "discharge planning," both as an aid to clinical management and to enhance clinical record keeping. If Dr. Johnson and his staff had full awareness of these concepts, there might have been less need for the dialogue which took place. In this context, it should be understood that legal commitment, by itself, is not sufficient to justify a hospital level of care to third-party payors.

Point of View: Psychiatry

In the foregoing dialogue, Dr. Johnson, the psychiatrist, approached the problem in a manner which included consideration of social and rehabilitative issues. His understanding of the nature and causes of the patient's illness and the goals of treatment included the involvement of the family as both contributing to and important in the resolution of the patient's illness. Even though the patient was relatively symptom-free during the latter part of her stay, he did not believe she could be returned to the pathogenic environment without a possible recurrence of her symptoms.

Clearly, Dr. Johnson found it difficult to fit his beliefs and perceptions of the patient's needs to the restrictive and unrealistic requirements of the health insurance company. He thus was impatient with the much more narrowly conceived medical model of Dr. Smith, the insurance company medical director. Dr. Johnson attempted to defend his treatment plan as being not only in the interest of the patient, but also cost-effective in reducing the chances of the patient's relapse and the family disturbance.

In contrast, Dr. Smith expressed the traditional medical view of the hospital as an institution for the dangerously disturbed patient and for treatment of serious illness which cannot be managed in any less intensive treatment setting. He sees two key elements to justify hospitalization: 1) "medical necessity" because of the seriousness of the patient's condition, and 2) rendering treatment to alleviate the condition which can only be performed in a hospital. This view focuses on acute illness, urgent need for care, and short-term treatment. It does not see, as a medical necessity, rehabilitation of chronic conditions or alleviation of problems in other areas of a patient's life.

Thus, in the perception of Dr. Smith, this girl had a temporary drug-induced psychosis from which she recovered quickly.

The fact that she was subsequently angry and depressed was, as he saw it, related to the fact that she was being kept in the hospital against her wishes.

Dr. Smith had considerable doubt about the medical necessity for her continued hospitalization because of the nursing notes from the latter part of Ms. Williams's hospitalization. In his mind, "medical necessity" does not include preventive, educational or rehabilitative measures, nor treatment of the disturbed family. Dr. Smith wondered if the diagnosis of "latent schizophrenia" was simply used to justify additional hospitalization, a concern reinforced by the fact that the patient was discharged just as benefits were about to run out.

In the dialogue, the viewpoints of both the clinical psychiatrist and the third-party insurer are presented in a vigorous and generally fair manner, although the rather aggressive approach of the medical director and the defensiveness of the clinical psychiatrist may not be typical.

The psychiatrist, Dr. Johnson, did not effectively communicate the rationale for his broad-based approach to the skeptical Dr. Smith, and the insurance company medical director was not helped to appreciate the differences between various types of psychiatric illness.

Dr. Johnson also failed to address effectively another important assumption which exists in both the public mind and in the minds of many physicians that psychiatric treatment is an endless process, a bottomless pit into which insurance money could be poured endlessly. Dr. Smith believes psychiatric hospitals routinely keep patients as long as insurance coverage permits, and that similar over-utilization will occur in day hospitals or outpatient treatment as well. This view may well stem from the chronicity of certain psychiatric illnesses and personality problems, and from the popular notion of interminable psychotherapy or psychoanalysis. The psychiatrist has to admit that this is a problem and help the critics understand the slow process of psychological change and the gradual workings of psychotherapy. In the dialogue, Dr. Johnson failed to deal with some of the assumptions expressed by Dr. Smith and, as a result, ended up reinforcing Dr. Smith's negative view about interminable psychiatric treatment.

Dr. Johnson summarized his position as follows: that the hospital must treat as long as necessary in order to allow the patient to return to her difficult home with a sufficient capability to avoid a future relapse. But this explanation was counterproductive when he implied that unless the insurance company broadens its coverage it is responsible for causing such patients again to have problems. This stance can only serve to polarize the position rather than to address the underlying assumptions behind Dr. Smith's position.

One of the problems in this dialogue is a preoccupation with diagnosis on the part of both of the physicians. This presents a problem because, in psychiatry as in some of the other medical specialties, patients are rarely hospitalized because of a specific diagnosis but, rather, to fulfill the treatment plan for the patient with that diagnosis. One commentator notes that it is not a diagnosis which justifies admission or continued hospitalization, but it is a treatment plan for symptoms manifested by the patient with the diagnosis. Thus, the diagnosis of mental disorder is not descriptive and does not necessarily indicate the need for clinical intervention. The need for a psychiatrist's care or hospitalization must be based on features other than the diagnosis itself.

Discussion

In addressing the kinds of differences reflected in the imaginary dialogue between Drs. Johnson and Smith, psychiatry must acknowledge some differences between psychiatric illness and general medical and surgical illnesses. Psychiatrists must be willing to admit that their approach to diagnosis is different instead of insisting that what they do is no different than treatment by the internist or surgeon. The psychiatrist also has to acknowledge that some of the therapies—particularly the psychotherapies—are something of a mystery to non-psychiatric physicians. For this reason, non-psychiatrists—and some psychiatrists—may doubt the efficacy or value of some treatments. Finally, psychiatrists must recognize that psychiatric care, both inpatient and outpatient, has generally not been subjected to the kind of peer review that would enhance its credibility.

Psychiatrists should see the implications of two potentially diverging paths. On the one hand, the profession may assert its medical identity, emphasizing parallels between psychiatric treatment and medical treatment, and diminish the psychotherapeutic aspects. On the other hand, the psychiatrist may seek public acceptance of a more broadly defined health perspective which might include forms of personal distress not now considered a medical illness.

The third-party payor also has certain responsibilities in this interaction. The psychiatrist may be justified in being upset by the third-party payor's response that a certain diagnosis would not warrant a long stay. Rather, what should have been communicated is something to the effect that "for such a length of stay, in addition to the diagnosis, we need more details about the patient's clinical status and the clinical treatment plan." That is, third-party payors should make it clear that the use of "duration of stay" norms for diagnostic groups does not fit standards or limitations for payment. Rather, it identifies those patients for whom additional clinical justification is necessary.

The third-party payor may also assist hospital staff in learning the concepts of "medical necessity," "level of care," and "discharge planning," and their relevance for case management and documentation.

With regard to the specific tactical errors evident in the interaction between Drs. Johnson and Smith, it is clear that each came to the meeting with his mind made up. Each seemed primarily concerned with defending his own position and was unable to hear the other side. While most psychiatrists might empathize with Dr. Johnson, psychiatrists must listen to and communicate more effectively with the Dr. Smiths of the world if they are to improve the standing of psychiatry with third-party payors. Psychiatrists need to know the history of insurance coverage as well as its economics. If Dr. Johnson had used a more intellectual rather than emotional approach, he might have anticipated most, if not all, of Dr. Smith's responses and countered the questions with facts.

As one of the reviewers noted, "There is most certainly an art of effective negotiating and the keystone is to develop the proper climate. In this dialogue, Dr. Johnson failed to do that. He should have been candid with Dr. Smith rather than questioning Smith's intelligence or the validity of his decision. One approach would have been to say, 'Dr. Smith, *we* have a problem. Your denial of part of Jane Williams's hospitalization at Pinecrest has serious consequences for me, the patient, and the hospital. It also creates ill will for your company with Jane, her family, and others. I would like your help in understanding the basis for your decision. I fully recognize your legal authority to make the decision. But since it does present serious consequences for all of us, I would like to explore ways to prevent similar outcomes in the future. I am sure you have good ideas that we could benefit from.'"

The reviewer added, "The most fruitful approach is to identify mutual problems and then establish a sincere and cooperative climate for resolving those problems. There is no doubt that Dr. Smith has good ideas, and had he been asked he would probably have quickly become an interested and involved participant. The greater the involvement, the greater the commitment toward finding an acceptable solution."

Another approach would be for Dr. Johnson to have initiated his discussions much earlier than he did. Perhaps he could have contacted Dr. Smith at the time Jane was reasonably recovered from the drug psychosis and asked his opinion on how to proceed. In other words, he could have initiated a form of concurrent review before charges occurred that might have precipitated questions from the insurance company. Dr. Smith sounded as if he suspected Dr. Johnson of attempting to hoodwink his insurance company into paying for services not covered by their policy. This distrust could be defused if problem cases such as this were discussed before the time benefit-review stage occurred. Chances are that such discussions would produce an accommodation that might not be entirely to Dr. Johnson's liking, but which would be better than the present impasse.

Effective communication only occurs when both parties are listening and attempting to understand. Both improve their understanding by being knowledgeable on all aspects of a topic, and both parties need to recognize the reality of the other's position and the right of the other individual to hold onto his or her position.

Psychiatrists attempting to negotiate with third-party payors must do their homework. They must be sensitive to the position of the insurance company, and be prepared to respond to the kinds of questions that are likely to arise. In addition, the psychiatrist must approach the insurer as a resource who has a legitimate concern about responding to the needs of its beneficiaries. The goal is to identify the mutual interest and to see if, through these interests, differences can be resolved and an optimal settlement achieved.

Clarifying the viewpoints of the psychiatrist to fellow physicians can be a problem even if the context is clinical, as Interface IV on the non-psychiatric physician suggests.

5

**INTERFACE IV
THE NON-PSYCHIATRIC PHYSICIAN**

Acknowledgments

We gratefully aknowledge the assistance of the following in the preparation of this chapter:

Jeremiah A. Barondess, *Clinical Professor, Department of Medicine, The New York Hospital, Cornell Medical Center; Past President, American College of Physicians, New York NY*

Merlin K. DuVal, *President, National Center for Health Education, San Francisco CA*

Maurice H. Greenhill, *Professor Emeritus of Psychiatry, Albert Einstein College of Medicine; Director of Psychiatry, The Hospital of Albert Einstein College of Medicine, New York NY (deceased)*

Thomas P. Hackett, *Draper Professor of Psychiatry, Harvard Medical School, Boston MA*

Don R. Lipsitt, *Associate Professor, Department of Psychiatry, Harvard Medical School; Chief of Psychiatry, Mount Auburn Hospital, Cambridge MA*

5

Interface IV

The Non-Psychiatric Physician

DIALOGUE

SETTING: The following dialogue takes place in a conference room of a general hospital where members of the medical staff are discussing the functions of the Department of Psychiatry in a general hospital setting.

PARTICIPANTS: Dr. Jones, Chairman—Department of Psychiatry
Dr. Smith, Chairman—Department of Pediatrics
Dr. Thompson, Chairman—Department of Medicine
Dr. Davis, Chairman—Department of Surgery
Dr. Brown, Chairman—Department of Plastic Surgery
Dr. Green, Chairman—Department of Family Practice
Dr. Starr, Chairman—Section of Proctology, Department of Surgery
Dr. Jackson, Chairman—Department of Obstetrics and Gynecology
Dr. Cohen, Chairman—Department of Ophthalmology
Dr. Bayle, Chairman—Department of Pathology

Dr. Jones (Psych): Our department furnishes the following services: consultation and liaison, outpatient treatment, short-term inpatient treatment, and day patient care. Are there any questions, comments or suggestions for improvement of any of these services?

Dr. Smith (Ped): All clinical departments offer consultations and accept referrals for transfer. What do you mean by consultation and liaison? How is this different from other consultative services?

Dr. Jones (Psych): Our liaison service is intended to assist non-psychiatrists in the ongoing management of the psychiatric problems of their patients. To facilitate this we are prepared to offer instruction to house officers, to nurses, and to other hospital employees who participate in patient care. When our liaison service works with a patient, we often involve members of several mental health professions who can contribute something to overall patient care. We coordinate psychiatric care with the other medical attention that the patient needs and provide ongoing help with managing the patient's emotional problems.

Dr. Thompson (Med): We don't want you to take over the care of our patients nor do we want you to instruct us in how to treat them. If we want continuing education, we'll sign up for the courses we want. What we want from you is your opinion about the psychiatric diagnosis, if any, what kind of treatment you recommend, what the prognosis is, and whether you will accept the patient for transfer to further inpatient or outpatient care when we are through with him or her.

Dr. Jones (Psych): You and your patient certainly aren't required to have ongoing involvement with our liaison staff simply because you request a consultation. If we think our continued participation will be helpful, we will recommend it. As with any other recommendation, you are free to accept it, not to accept it, or get another opinion. Our intention is to be helpful, and not to be intrusive.

Dr. Thompson (Med): Even when you answer a consultation request in a regular way, some of your staff give me all sorts of gobbledygook about dynamics, and a review of the patient's unhappy childhood, together with some stuff about the stresses he or she has been experiencing. It may be interesting to some people, but it isn't anything I can use.

Dr. Davis (Surg): There is one thing that I would like to know when I request a consultation. I recognize that some of my patients are nervous, depressed, or even paranoid, but I would like to know whether these conditions are primary psychiatric disorders, secondary to the disease process which I am treating, or even if it's just the reaction of a patient to being sick.

Dr. Brown (Pl Surg): I want to know how the psychiatric disorder influences the medical and surgical management of patients. I really don't care all that much about the psychiatric diagnosis. I want to know if the patient is stable enough for an elective procedure. Like, I know he's nervous, but is the nose job he is asking for contraindicated; will it help him or will he go psychotic if it turns out badly?

Dr. Jones (Psych): Your points are well taken. You want specific information and we should supply it. It would help, of course, if you indicated the specific questions you have in mind when you request the consultation. However, even if you don't, we should include the things you mentioned at the beginning of our reports. If we go ahead and tell you something about the makeup of the patient that goes beyond what you have asked, or about the psychosocial stressors that he or she has encountered, it is with the hope that this will help you understand him or her better, but if it is going to be useful, we should certainly put it in plain language and not in the jargon of our trade.

Dr. Green (Fam Prac): I have read that you spend more than twice as long with each patient as is spent by the average family doctor or internist. Is this time well spent? Is it cost-effective? Or is it only to justify higher fees?

Dr. Jones (Psych): On the average we *do* spend more time because we need a more detailed life history from new patients, and because certain techniques of psychotherapy are time-consuming. However, for certain patients in routine office visits, especially when the patient is complying with medication, we spend no more time than any other doctor. Sometimes spending more time on each appointment in a scheduled series of appointments saves time in the long run because the patient spends less time in treatment than if he or she made many more short visits and calls.

Dr. Smith (Ped): Will you make more use of medicine in the future and spend less time on psychoanalysis and other such time-consuming aberrations? Can't you do as we do: write the prescription; and, if the patient needs counseling, find a social worker?

Dr. Jones (Psych): Medication plays an important role in the treatment of patients with psychiatric disorders but in itself, it is not enough for many of our patients. This is true of certain other patients who do not usually come to see psychiatrists. For example, prescribing medication and giving dietary advice to a diabetic or a hypertensive does not cure or control the disorder unless the patient takes the medicine and follows the advice. An internist may need to spend quite a lot of time finding out the reasons for noncompliance before real progress in treatment can be made. We have similar problems in getting patients to continue to take needed medication, and we also need to help them explore personal problems and their ways of life. We utilize the services of other mental health professionals too. These persons must be adequately trained and adequately supervised. Some of them can indeed do psychotherapy. However, care for the sick patient, even care that employs techniques that can readily be learned by the layman, requires ongoing attention to differential diagnosis and to the overall health of the patient.

Dr. Starr (Proc): People who write to "Dear Abby" are often told to get counseling. Do you think that sort of thing benefits people or wouldn't it be better for them to be independent and handle their own problems?

Dr. Jackson (Ob/Gyn): One of my patients whom I didn't realize had a psychiatric problem wrote to "Dear Abby," but she was not told to get counseling. She was told to see a psychiatrist. She did, and it helped her. As far as helping oneself is concerned, it would be good to remember that this is no longer the wild frontier, and we do not have to do everything ourselves. When someone needs the help of an expert, they should get it.

Dr. Davis (Surg): The psychiatrists here are almost as good as real doctors, but I know some in the community who are crazier than the patients they treat. How can people with problems of their own help others?

Dr. Jones (Psych): Good mental health is important for any physician. Some psychiatric conditions are disabling and physicians who have them should not practice pending adequate treatment. On the other hand, many conditions do not interfere with one's work, and having some problems may make it easier for the psychiatrist to understand the feelings of patients. You don't need to have a baby to be a good obstetrician, but it might help. Likewise, having experienced the heartbreak of psoriasis does not incapacitate a dermatologist for treating the itch.

Dr. Thompson (Med): Isn't the overuse of tranquilizers, especially benzodiazepines, almost like drug abuse? Aren't too many patients popping pills? Shouldn't people be able to tolerate some discomfort in living?

Dr. Jones (Psych): It is true that a high percentage of American people in all social classes take psychoactive medicine sometime during each year. Some patients do misuse these medications but most do not. Studies of patients who have been given minor tranquilizers and furnished them on request while in a psychiatric ward show that the majority of patients do not overuse the drugs. It is one of the duties of the physician to relieve discomfort whenever he or she can. Certainly, we do not want to over-prescribe. We need to be alert and to detect the occasional patient who is likely to become habituated to symptomatic medication. However, just because a few patients misuse medication doesn't mean that we should deny relief to the much greater number who do not. We shouldn't let any personal moral position regarding the horror of the recreational use of drugs interfere with the practice of medicine.

Dr. Cohen (Ophth): We had a patient in for eye surgery not long ago who clearly was mentally ill; his conduct on the ward created real problems for the nurses. Miss Quigley, who has been at this hospital for over thirty years, was so upset by his repeated immoral propositions that she had to go off duty. His family says that he is bankrupting himself by reckless expenditures. Your residents said that he was manic, which I don't doubt, but they refused to transfer him to the psychiatric ward without his consent. When I asked to have your resident disciplined I got nowhere.

Dr. Jones (Psych): Under the laws of this state, a patient cannot be committed or admitted to any psychiatric facility without his or her consent unless the Mental Health Board finds that the patient is dangerous either to himself or others. Danger means an immediate overt threat of bodily harm. It does *not* include wasting money or making improper propositions to Miss Quigley. If he had threatened to murder or rape Miss Quigley it would have been different. Then involuntary hospitalization could have been recommended. It might be better if we had a law that recognized mental illness together with incompetence for decision-making on one's own behalf as a basis for hospitalization, but that is not the way it is.

Dr. Cohen (Ophth): I see that I will have to give that patient's family a short lecture on Forensic Psychiatry.

Dr. Thompson (Med): Members of your staff frequently testify in criminal cases. How can a psychiatrist tell if a patient was insane at the time of a crime? If a criminal is sent to a psychiatric hospital, how do you know that he is cured or rehabilitated before he is released? If there are scientific measures of sanity, how can two equally renowned psychiatrists come to opposite conclusions in the courtroom?

Dr. Jones (Psych): Insanity is a legal and not a medical concept. The disagreements in court are usually not about diagnosis or the mental state at the time of the crime which can usually be determined from the patient's condition at the time of examination and verifiable history, but the degree to which the patient fits legal definitions. Many psychiatrists have advocated determining the facts of the case first and not utilizing the defense "not guilty by reason of insanity," but taking the criminal's condition into account in planning for treatment and rehabilitation after determination of guilt or innocence. In regard to the discharge of the mentally ill person who has committed a crime, we can't be sure that a person who committed a crime while mentally ill will never commit another one any more than we can be sure that a person who served his time in a penitentiary, without ever having been mentally ill, won't commit more crimes. One discharges a patient when he or she is well or is in adequate remission, and obviously, arrangements for longterm follow-up are desirable. Often such arrangements do not exist. In a free society we don't confine a person indefinitely for what he or she might do; rather, we try to prevent harm to others. A particular problem occurs with some sex offenders who have few, if any, symptoms aside from deviant sexual impulses. If such a person is confined and has no opportunity to act on such impulses, we can't be sure what he or she might do outside the hospital or prison. As an alternative to lifetime confinement for a person who has not committed an offense meriting such confinement, we must allow some freedom while ensuring adequate supervision.

Dr. Bayle (Path): Most, if not all biological theories dealing with the etiology of schizophrenia or depression, are extrapolated from drug effects and essentially are pharmacologically originated. Why doesn't the mental health profession have any new insights into the etiology of mental illness?

Dr. Jones (Psych): I don't know the answer to that question but I do know that research expenditure per year for each patient under care for schizophrenia equals about $7.35 compared to $203.16 for each cancer patient and $88.16 for each cardiac patient. Our friends in the government say that you can't solve a problem by "throwing money at it," but throwing a little more money at this problem might, through research findings, save a great deal of money, not to mention suffering, in the future.

Dr. Smith (Ped): Why don't you do more about prevention?

Dr. Jones (Psych): Effective techniques in prevention cannot be developed without additional research, including adequate demonstration projects. Large-scale attempts at preventing mental illness and improving mental health based on theory alone are a waste of tax money. Both research and preventive activities are difficult to undertake in a setting like ours where reimbursement to a large extent is on the basis of a fee-for-service system from third-party payors. This arrangement has many advantages in the delivery of patient care services but the public, through government agencies, must, in the long run, undertake programs in research and in preventive medicine. The only other option for funding these activities would be for third-party payors to contribute a portion of fees for such purposes, and that isn't likely to happen.

Overview

This conference illustrates many of the problems that arise between a psychiatry chairman and his colleagues. One is tempted to analyze the communication in terms of its substance; yet the more cogent issues are process issues. Communication can be analyzed in terms of *who* says what *to whom* and in what context. The "who" is a psychiatrist who is an administrative department head. The "to whom" is a group of other administrative department heads who are not psychiatric physicians. Barriers to communication are hardly confined to relationships between psychiatrists and their non-psychiatric colleagues. Physicians in general do not communicate readily with one another. Medical schools do not spend much time selecting students for their communicative skills nor do they spend time remedying defects in these skills. Psychiatrists learn specific interviewing and psychotherapy techniques which may be inappropriate in the context of communication within a conference with other department heads. It is all too easy to forget the context of the communication and fall back on communication methods more appropriate to the consulting room or the classroom.

The demand characteristics for this communication are set in the opening comments. The psychiatry chairman, Dr. Jones, gave a one-sentence list of services followed by, "Are there any questions, comments, or suggestions for improvement of any of these services?" This is a nice open-ended question metaphorically akin to the "say anything that comes to mind" of an analytic hour, but inappropriate within the context of an administrative conference. The hostile reactions that ensued are not surprising. Communications within meetings of busy department chairmen should be goal-directed. While brevity is desirable, it is no substitute for specificity.

Nonetheless, the ensuing comments provided ample opportunities for illustrating some basic communication problems between psychiatrists, non-psychiatrists and non-psychiatric physicians.

Point of View: Non-Psychiatric Physicians

Unlike most psychiatrists, the non-psychiatric physician operates from a different perspective. This position has evolved from the remarkable flowering of biomedical science and technology over the past three decades. As a consequence, there has emerged a view of diseases based on a sophisticated cellular and molecular biology providing for the first time, a truly scientific base for much of clinical medicine. The task of understanding the mass of information which comes from medical research now dominates medical school curricula. To an ever increasing degree, physicians have evolved the view that understanding the patient's *disease* in pathophysiologic and, if possible, molecular terms is a prime characteristic of the well-conducted clinical transaction. Education and training time devoted to the components, characteristics, and management of the human being who feels ill has been neglected.

Psychiatrists, in contrast, have developed a paradigm in which the clinical focus is the discomfort, the psychosocial disruption, perceptions, and formulations of the patient. There is far less emphasis on the biomedical model and much more understanding of the patient's agenda rather than the doctor's agenda. While it is true that there has been a gradual return of the biological and the medical model to psychiatry so that the use of medication now resembles other medical specialties, there remain substantial differences.

One of these differences is traceable to basic dissimilarities in attacking a clinical problem, even when both are working within the so-called "medical model." It is not merely rooted in the inherent pitfalls of the mind/body dualism. The non-psychiatrist is accustomed to starting with the traditional chief complaint and directing his efforts "centripetally" toward a narrower and narrower focus which he hopes will yield not only a diagnosis but also a suspected etiology. Balint has termed this the "illness-oriented" approach. The psychiatrist, on the other hand, starting with the same chief complaint, will work "centrifugally" through the interview process to enlarge upon the chief complaint. This encompasses broader and broader circles of influence upon the patient which may ultimately provide sufficient intrapsychic, interpersonal, social, genetic, economic, familial, and occupational data essential to a formulation. The assumption is that the dysfunction is multidetermined and that the symptom is but a signal or a cue. Balint calls this the "patient-oriented" appoach.

These approaches also stem from different data bases. The data base in modern medicine is increasingly precise: it utilizes measuring instruments which produce replicable data, and employs the tools of molecular biology, biochemistry, and biophysics. In cases where psychiatry utilizes a similar data base (as in measures of neurotransmitters in schizophrenia), communication is much easier. On the other hand, the data base of psychiatry is quite different, emphasizing natural observation of life history, generalizations about social phenomena, and reliance on psychodynamics and interpretation.

In turn, a great disparity in terms of the precision of communication is created. Communication in non-psychiatric medicine is usually precise and to the point. In contrast, communication about psychosocial issues often seems unduly vague.

There are parallel issues of time. The psychiatric time frame may be marked in weeks, months, or years. The units of time on a busy medical/surgical service are marked in minutes and hours. Open-ended general discussion may, in the long run, be the most rapid method to determine truth with reference to a psychiatric patient. The same communication is viewed as wasteful and even disrespectful on a medical service.

Different styles of communication then become apparent. Perhaps the most telling example of this stylistic difference is the tendency of the psychiatrist to interpret disagreement by non-psychiatric physicians as evidence of unconscious resistance. This may, in fact, be quite true; nonetheless, participants in discussions about the nature of an allied service rarely come with the intent of having their unconscious resistances identified for public scrutiny. The psychiatrist may be accustomed to withstanding a great deal of hostility without responding and may, in fact, even assume a stance of benign superiority in the face of attack. A harried surgeon may prefer an angry human response to an omniscient smile.

Even the specific language used may be quite different. Increased specialization contributes to the evolution of specialized languages so that even the same bodily events may be described in parallel languages, each undecipherable to the other specialist.

All these issues are brought out in the dialogue. The psychiatrist begins the dialogue by telling us essentially nothing. The list of services he provides is identical to what every other clinical department provides except for the addition of day care and liaison services, neither of which is defined or explained. When he was asked what a liaison service is, he informed us that he is prepared to offer education to hospital employees

The Non-Psychiatric Physician

(presumably us) and that he will come around with members of several mental health professions. In that context, the internist's sharp negative response was understandable. He provided what is to the non-psychiatric physician a reasonable response to a consultation request. The psychiatrist gave another non-specific, defensive reply and there followed three comments by different non-psychiatric physicians about the jargon being used on the psychiatric service; the lack of clarity about the nature of reactions to sickness and operative procedures and the need for information about how psychiatric disorders influence medical and surgical management. None of the questions were answered. The psychiatrist concurred that the "points are well taken. You want specific information; we should supply it." However, he supplied *no* specific information.

This portion of the dialogue raises very basic issues about the consultation process. The etiquette of consultation is widely accepted among non-psychiatric physicians. Consultation does not mean turning a patient over to another service unless there is mutual agreement that this is in the patient's best interest. There is inherent anxiety in the consultation process in that the physician's diagnosis and management may be criticized. Each time an internist asks a colleague to evaluate some specific part of the treatment plan, he may invite an indictment of the care he is rendering. Moreover, as multiple consultants become involved, there may be a loss of control over the patient's care. Finally, there is always a danger that some of the consultants will "stir up" the patient and/or the family, making the job of the primary physician more difficult. So long as consultation is offered within the basic framework of medical practice which involves evaluation, diagnosis, recommended treatment, and probable prognosis and availability of ongoing consultation, a certain order is brought into the consultative process. When psychiatric consultation is rendered days late in language which is undecipherable and in a format which is not understandable, all of the rules of consultation are broken. When consultation means that a Cecil B. DeMille cast arrives complete with psychologists, social worker, psychiatric nurse, rehab counselor, and supporting players, the consultation may be too much of an ordeal to endure. The comments in the dialogue reflected the disparity between the expectations of the non-psychiatric physician and that which psychiatrists often deliver in general hospitals. The remainder of the dialogue showed continuing deterioration in the level of communication. It was obvious that Dr. Jones's non-psychiatric colleagues were not just hostile but directly angry in their comments and behavior.

Point of View: Psychiatry

Even allowing for our dramatic overstatement, Dr. Jones, the psychiatrist, did not emerge from this trying conference covered with any particular glory. During the conference, Dr. Jones absorbed such insulting remarks as, "The psychiatrists here are almost as good as real doctors, but I know some in the community who are crazier than the patients they treat." He listened imperviously to statements identifying psychodynamics as "gobbledygook," reviews of unhappy childhood experiences as a waste of time, and "stuff about the stresses" the patient experiences as equally useless. The conference was characterized by an adversary tone and a clearly hostile atmosphere.

The first response which the psychiatric physician may make to the dialogue is that it should never have occurred at all. The dialogue accurately depicted the ineffectiveness of medical education in preparing non-psychiatric physicians to deal with the psychosocial aspects of medical care. If medical schools ever provide a program of continuous reinforcement concerning learning and acquisition of skills in the psychology of medical practice, programs of mandatory (evaluated) training in interview skills, etc., conferences like this may not take place.

In the interim, the role of psychiatrist is indeed different from other specialists. The unpleasant truth is that the consulting psychiatrist must do things in addition to those done by other specialist consultants. The psychiatrist in a general hospital does engage in consultation with reference to such psychiatric illnesses as depressions, schizophrenic reactions, organic brain syndromes, etc. In addition, the psychiatrist is often called upon to deal with the emotional problems resulting from treatment of somatic disease.

A psychiatrist in the general hospital must carry out multiple and, at times, conflicting roles. Obviously, he functions as a representative of a specialty of medicine. The chief of the psychiatry service also functions as one of the administrators in administrative meetings. There are additional roles of teacher and, at times, of preacher which are likely to evoke a great deal of hostility unless they are practiced with extreme compassion, tact, and sensitivity. Our advice to Dr. Jones is to give up the preacher's role entirely. Moreover, there is a distinction between being an effective teacher and being a pedant. Lecturettes in administrative meetings are a poor idea. The main method of teaching in liaison psychiatry must be by constant interchange with colleagues in clinical situations. From the tone of the meeting, one gathers that Dr. Jones had not spent sufficient time mingling with his fellow chairmen. The most effective means of communication is on a one-to-one informal basis. Most of the topics covered in this meeting should never have come up. Some would have been rendered unnecessary if the psychiatrist functioned more effectively in a liaison capacity. Several guidelines may help to render the liaison role more effective.

- Mingle with other specialists as often as possible. This means not only at Grand Rounds, formal committees and society meetings, but also at the lunch table, informal walking rounds, and the coffee room.

• Be available. The effective liaison psychiatrist operates on the surgeon's clock. Requests for consultation should be answered quickly, and psychiatrists need to be as available as members of other specialty groups.

• Work outward from within medical models. This means being sensitive to where the non-psychiatric physician begins. Lectures from an internist on the nature of consultation shouldn't be necessary. The artificial dichotomy between psychiatry and non-psychiatric medicine is equally undesirable. The psychiatrist works both from biotechnical models and psychosocial models. What differentiates the psychiatrist from other mental health professionals is the psychiatrist's familiarity with medical models. While it is true that psychiatry needs to be patient-oriented in the Balint sense, the psychiatrist should be equally at home using medical language and understanding disease processes. The approaches are not mutually exclusive. Adequate practice of medicine requires both approaches, not only with psychiatric patients, but with all medical patients.

• Consultation notes should be succinct, legible, comprehensible, and practical. The recommendations, insofar as possible, should lend themselves to implementation by non-psychiatrists and should fit into their practice format. If referral was suggested, careful explanation of the reasons for the recommendation would diffuse any criticisms of "patient snatching," and detailed suggestions about how to refer will facilitate the physician's task. Consultation notes should not be long or rambling. It is an unusual request that requires more than a handwritten page in reply. A statement of the problem, the diagnosis, a reason to substantiate the diagnosis, and a suggested plan are what is needed. The presence of jargon is absolutely contraindicated in a consultation note.

• Preaching and interpretation of other physicians' behavior have no place in a general hospital. The psychiatrist must remember that his colleagues are not requesting consultation for or diagnosis of themselves. The psychiatrist should avoid being preachy to his non-psychiatrist colleagues. A large part of the skill of communicating with others about psychiatry is to choose one's words carefully, to generalize from common examples, and to minimize distortion and mystification by being straightforward and clear. The utmost in tact, sensitivity, humility, and a spirit of helpfulness are called for.

However, even the most skilled liaison psychiatrist functioning with colleagues who are reasonably sophisticated about psychosocial care may still run into a difficult administrative conference. In this example, the psychiatrist made the mistake of confusing an administrative meeting with a medical school classroom teaching situation. While interpretations of other people's behavior are contraindicated in administrative conferences the psychiatrist should not forget the skills he has acquired in dealing with process issues. How does one communicate clearly and effectively in administrative conferences? These principles should help:

• *Identify conference goals clearly and make sure comments are directed to these goals.* In this conference, the psychiatrist lacked a clear task orientation. He let the conference get away from him by comments which were far too open-ended. Given the physicians he was dealing with, the open-ended beginning evoked hostility. In general, administrative conferences involve exchanges of information relevant to the entire hospital staff and decision-making concerning policy, space, budget, or the external boundaries of the hospital. Psychiatrists in chairmanship positions need to identify common interests with other department chairmen. At times, territorial conflict occurs, and in such settings the psychiatrist needs to be skilled in building alliances and in gaining support. Because the conference goals were so vague in the dialogue, one cannot tell what this psychiatry chairman was trying to achieve.

- *Be prepared for status conflicts.* It is difficult to know what the nature of the status conflict was in this conference. Were there issues about space or budget which influenced the other department chairmen, or did they come by their hostility gratuitously? Even the most skilled chairman will, from time to time, find himself in confrontation with more powerful departments. Our advice to chairmen in this situation is, "Do your homework." This means establishing alliances and making proper compromises before the administrative conference begins. When a psychiatry chairman is subjected to the type of humiliating remarks that were made in this conference, it probably means that the status of psychiatry in that hospital is about to take another sharp turn downward.

- *Pay attention to administrative process issues.* The psychiatrist in the dialogue behaved like a "rational actor" in what sounded like a rather irrational conference. When the process becomes unduly hostile, what does one do? Well, don't try a psychiatric interpretation of the process to anyone except yourself. Once you make that interpretation to yourself, there are things that you can do. Some have found it highly effective to introduce humor to defuse a rather charged process, so long as offensive ridicule is avoided. Others have found it most effective to deal with the underlying process through explanation of the issues. Such explanations can only be useful in a non-hostile environment. For example, Dr. Jones's excursions into forensics and other topics won him no respite. In general, hostile statements should not go unchallenged, even if the challenge is only in the form of humor or a brief comment. Questions should not be permitted to pile up on top of each other as they did in this conference.

At a minimum, the process of this conference should have provided Dr. Jones with evidence that he has a great deal of work to do. He probably could arrange individual meetings over lunch or in some informal setting with each of the involved chairmen and discuss these comments in much greater detail. In these individual encounters, Dr. Jones should try to get behind the generalities to specifics and find out what's really been going on.

Discussion

The psychiatrist functioning in a general hospital setting must remember his own medical origins and understand from the beginning the style, viewpoint, and values of his colleagues. Perhaps effective medical education will increasingly build bridges between disease orientation and patient orientation. In the absence of such bridges, non-psychiatric physicians may attack the approach of the psychiatrist. The best place to deal with such issues is not in an administrative conference, but in day-to-day work on the wards, at Grand Rounds, and at the bedside. An effective consultation/liaison service should go far toward mitigating the problem. Psychiatric consultation should be characterized by ready availability of a psychiatrist who is able to operate within medical models, write succinct practical notes, and share meaningful collegiality.

Administrative conferences require task orientation and proper goal setting. The psychiatrist addressing an administrative conference should have some sense of his proper administrative role. He should not leave behind communication skills such as humor and effective interchange. In the conference described, things had already gone too far. The proper setting for dealing with this level of hostility is not in conference, but in informal meetings with the other chairmen. Faced with an unpleasant meeting such as this one, the psychiatrist should retain his sense of humor, his dignity, and a certain unwillingness to have his field disparaged.

Presenting his case before a predominantly lay group may be just as much of a challenge to the psychiatrist as presenting it to other physicians, as Interface V on the health planner illustrates.

6

**INTERFACE V
THE HEALTH PLANNER**

Acknowledgments

We gratefully acknowledge the assistance of the following in the preparation of this chapter:

Joanne Finley, *Commissioner, Department of Health, State of New Jersey, Trenton NJ*

Robert W. Gibson, *Medical Director, The Sheppard and Enoch Pratt Hospital, Towson MD*

Theresa M. Hottenroth, *Planner, Southeastern Wisconsin Health Systems Agency, Milwaukee WI*

Russell E. Julian, *Executive Director, Southeastern Wisconsin Health Systems Agency, Milwaukee WI*

N. Karen Kelly, *Chairman of Planning, Allegheny County HSA; Chairman, Citizens Board, Western Pennsylvania Psychiatric Institute and Clinic, Pittsburgh PA*

Jannie Milt, *Executive Director, The Mental Health Association in New Jersey, Montclair NJ*

Richard G. Morrill, *Clinical Director, Erich Lindemann Mental Health Center; Assistant Professor of Psychiatry, Harvard Medical School, Boston MA*

William Newman, *Former Executive Director, Northeast Kansas Health Systems Agency, Topeka KS*

6

Interface V

The Health Planner

DIALOGUE

SETTING: A psychiatrist is presenting his hospital's application for additional inpatient beds to a Health Systems Agency (HSA) Committee. He is a knowledgeable psychiatrist and understands the modern care of the mentally ill, including the focus of providing a treatment alternative that is least restrictive. The Chairman of the Committee is quite knowledgeable about mental health issues, and the Committee has had previous experience with review of proposals for psychiatric services.

PARTICIPANTS: Dr. Martin—Hospital Psychiatrist
Mr. Jones—Chairman of Health Systems Agency Committee
Mr. Thomas—Member, HSA Committee
Mrs. Smith—Member, HSA Committee
Mrs. Rogers—Member, HSA Committee
Mr. Brown—Member, HSA Committee

Dr. Martin: I would like to take this opportunity to thank you for granting us the privilege of presenting our Certificate of Need for additional inpatient beds. We have done a careful needs assessment in our catchment area and have determined that the additional 20 beds we are requesting would be adequately utilized. Our studies show that our inpatient census has been at 100 percent occupancy for 25 out of the 30 days of each month, necessitating our turning away patients from our own catchment area as well as refusing patients from other catchment areas. We have not always been able to find alternative beds, particularly for many of our chronically ill patients, and several tragedies may have occurred as a result of this.

Mr. Jones: You say several tragedies have occurred?

Dr. Martin: Yes. There have been two suicides among patients we were unable to place. Although one cannot be sure, these might have been averted had there been beds available.

Mr. Jones: You point out that your beds are full most of the time. Can you prove that all those hospitalizations are really necessary?

Dr. Martin: I am glad you asked, because I have submitted material to you which has been prepared by our Utilization Review Committee. The Committee has disallowed some days, but in general we have a pretty good record. Our average length of stay for our 90-bed unit is 20 days and, out of 32,760 patient days, only 655 were disallowed by the Utilization Review Committee. These were most often elderly patients for whom a placement was difficult to find. Only seven total admissions were disallowed by the Committee.

Mr. Thomas: Are all the other inpatient units this busy or are you the exception?

Dr. Martin: I have statistics to show that all the psychiatric units in our county have similar occupancy rates. We have documentation that shows no available beds in 82 percent of the calls we made over a six-month period. Of course, we realize that some units are not anxious to take some of our patients.

Mrs. Smith: Why would some hospitals be unwilling to take certain of your patients?

Dr. Martin: A large number of our patients are indigent and without family support systems; it may be difficult to find a place for them to return to in the community. We try to take that responsibility but it doesn't always work. Many of our patients are chronically ill, and we have quite a few violent individuals admitted, sometimes brought by the police. General hospital units in some of the catchment areas would rather not take these patients. Our contract with the county requires us to accept these patients if we have beds.

Mr. Jones: Dr. Martin, we have read about alternative types of treatment programs for the psychiatric patient, such as partial hospitalization. Would it be possible to fill your needs if you developed more partial hospital slots or positions?

Dr. Martin: Your question is reasonable. I know that the psychiatric literature often points out that a day hospital may be a very effective alternative to 24-hour care. That, of course, refers to the ideal day hospital and not to the usual one in our community.

Mrs. Rogers: What do you mean by that?

Dr. Martin: If a day hospital is to serve as an alternative to 24-hour inpatient care, it should be located in, or have available the services of, a general hospital. Many of the so-called day hospitals in our community are freestanding. They do not relate directly to a general hospital and really do not offer all the services you need to be an effective alternative to 24-hour care.

Mrs. Rogers: Why would a psychiatric day hospital need to relate to a general hospital? What kind of services does this kind of program need?

Dr. Martin: All patients coming into a care system need to undergo a thorough assessment process. One of the places where this assessment can be obtained is in the hospital as an inpatient. Here, the necessary evaluation, including psychological testing, a general medical examination, laboratory tests, and any special studies which may be needed are carried out. Unless one is in a special psychiatric unit or closely affiliated with one where these various assessment tools are available, it is impossible to use that facility as an alternative to inpatient care. In fact, it is a disservice to the patient to fail to assess him or her as accurately and as fully as possible.

Mr. Jones: Can't this be done as an outpatient, using the hospital facilities?

Dr. Martin: Certainly, but I thought we were talking about patients who were too disturbed to be handled as outpatients, who need either inpatient or day hospital care.

Mr. Jones: Well then, if we limit our discussion to the severely disturbed patient, did you say that the majority of day hospitals in this area cannot do the assessment?

Dr. Martin: That's right. I should explain that I don't think many of them actually are day hospitals, but are really day care facilities where people who have been assessed and really do not need hospital care can go to daily programs as they make an adjustment in the community. Most of their patients have been released from hospitals, have residual or chronic emotional disturbances and are not ready for outpatient treatment.

Don't misunderstand what I am saying. I believe that day care facilities are very important. The patient in need of therapeutic recreation, social skills development, assertiveness training, medication monitoring, etc., will benefit a great deal from such facilities. That type of individual would not need the more intensive evaluation and treatment facilities of the "true" day hospital.

The Health Planner 105

Mr. Brown: You sound enthusiastic about the potential for day hospital programs to treat the seriously disturbed patient. However, I'm not clear about the differences in admission criteria between a day hospital and an inpatient program.

Dr. Martin: A good question. Surprisingly, the reasons for admission to day hospital and 24-hour inpatient care are very similar if the day hospital is of the intensive type with a full range of hospital services. The basic differences are as follows:

> If a patient is clearly suicidal or homicidal or has made serious threats regarding either, he should be under 24-hour care with close observation. If the threats are vague and the danger is judged to be low, and if there is a responsible family to care for the patient, then we might consider a day hospital. If the patient is extremely disorganized in his thinking, 24-hour inpatient care is indicated. As the patient improves, day hospital would be considered. These decisions will depend on the degree of disorganization, the strength of the social supports, and the patient's control over his behavior.
>
> The family is crucial to the success of day hospital placement; the family must be willing to have the patient at home and neither the patient nor the family should be seriously destructive of each other.
>
> Cases of severe brain damage, and many cases of alcoholism or drug addiction which require withdrawal or other medical intervention, should be treated in a 24-hour hospital.
>
> Transportation problems must be solved if a patient is to be placed in a day hospital, and this usually depends on the family's cooperation.
>
> The patient may move from one program to the other as need dictates if both programs exist in the same care system. A day hospital patient may require admission to inpatient care if

the illness intensifies or complications develop. Likewise, an inpatient may be discharged to a day hospital after a brief hospitalization before he would be ready for outpatient treatment. Does this answer your question?

Mr. Brown: Yes, the distinctions seem clearer now. Does your institution have a day hospital program?

Dr. Martin: No, we don't.

Mr. Jones: You seem to be quite positive about the usefulness of the day hospital program as part of an integrated treatment delivery system.

Dr. Martin: Well, yes. I think it definitely has a contribution to make.

Mr. Jones: With what you've told us, why aren't you asking for a day hospital facility in your current Certificate of Need?

Dr. Martin: Because we feel that there is a great need for 24-hour beds in our area. An additional 20 beds would probably meet the current demand for inpatient beds in our county.

Mr. Jones: I get the feeling that there is something more to it than you are saying. You're asking us to approve enlargement of your psychiatric unit to 110 beds, while you don't have any day hospital facilities at all. I have a feeling you're not leveling with us.

Dr. Martin: I am. I will admit, however, if there was a way to pay for a *good* day hospital program, we would probably be asking for a split, say 10 new inpatient beds and 15 day hospital slots.

Mr. Jones: You'll have to explain further what you mean.

Dr. Martin: In all honesty, there is a financial premium on 24-hour beds. All third-party payors cover costs for inpatient beds, but pay very little for day hospital care.

Mr. Thomas: Can you be more precise about the reimbursement rates?

Dr. Martin: Yes. They pay about $25.00 a day, while it would cost nearly $75.00 a day for a good program. You go broke following that scale, or else end up with an inadequate program. We would like to develop a day hospital, but would need a more realistic payment rate before we could do so. The insurance companies just aren't realistic about reimbursement rates and won't listen to the hospital's point of view.

Mr. Jones: You have started me thinking about it. Perhaps our HSA could join others in the state in lobbying for better payment for day hospitals. It would certainly seem to be a cost-effective approach. We would need to work closely with the hospitals and community mental health centers to develop a united front. Do you think we can count on them for cooperation?

Dr. Martin: Yes, I'm certain of it. Please remember that a day hospital can't solve all our current problems, but it would certainly help in bringing the costs down. It must be coordinated with adequate inpatient facilities.

Mr. Jones: I think we should talk more about your suggestion to reduce your request to 10 inpatient beds, but I would like to see them linked to a day hospital program. I think our Committee would be more favorable to that kind of comprehensive system. We'll also see about forming a coalition for better day hospital reimbursement.

Dr. Martin: I can get a group from the providers to join with you in such a coalition, but the efforts of citizens' groups such as yours will be essential if we want to influence insurance regulations.

Mr. Jones: I feel confident we can get the HSAs behind it.

Dr. Martin: I hope we can get to work on it soon. Our county desperately needs such a program if our inpatient beds are going to be limited. We will reevaluate our proposal for inpatient beds in light of your suggested limit of 10 beds, and will consider the feasibility of developing a day hospital program. Thanks for your attention and interest, and let's hope our coalition idea succeeds.

Point of View: Health Systems Agency Committee

This dialogue represents an encounter between a psychiatrist and a new type of institution, the citizen-dominated corporation, designed to regulate health-care institutions and professions. During the past two decades, the public has become increasingly distrustful of the ability of professions, hospitals, schools and government agencies to regulate health care. Following the model of public education, recent federal legislation has established an array of local, regional and statewide organizations to regulate and plan for health care in the public interest. Psychiatry, like the rest of medicine, has generally been resistant to this encroachment on its traditional autonomy, and few psychiatrists have become knowledgeable about, and far fewer involved with, this planning process. The first requirement for any involvement with such agencies is a knowledge of their structure, process and goals.

The current health planning system was established by the National Health Planning and Resources Development Act of 1974. This act established a nationwide program of health planning and resource allocation with the goal of providing all citizens equal access to quality health care at a reasonable cost. The cornerstone of this system is the Health Systems Agency (HSA), a regional body of volunteer consumers (citizens) and providers (anyone involved in health care delivery), which must have a majority of consumers on its governing boards and committees.

It should be recognized that the dialogue under discussion presents an atypical HSA committee (it has no providers), probably to highlight the conflicts which often occur betwen lay members of HSA's and psychiatrists. Similarly, the presence of providers on HSA committees can facilitate resolution of conflicts.

A general goal of HSAs is to substitute ambulatory and intermediate care for inpatient services. Another goal is to avoid new inpatient beds if there are underutilized beds in the same institution, or in other nearby institutions providing the same services. The HSA has little leverage to eliminate existing underutilized or unnecessary beds. Instead, it has tried to restrain the addition of new beds and thereby force the transfer of underutilized beds to services with emerging needs.

In an actual situation, the HSA Review Committee will have already received the statistics which Dr. Martin gave orally. It will also have received a careful analysis of the need factors, financial feasibility, and possible alternatives to the proposal. The possibility of substituting day hospital slots for inpatient beds would most probably have already been considered by the HSA staff.

As mentioned earlier, the HSA Review Committee encountered by Dr. Martin in this dialogue is by no means typical of the committees one encounters in actual HSAs, since most such groups are larger and much more diverse in the make-up and attitudes of their members. (This, however, does not mean that the conflicts portrayed do not occur.) Participation in an HSA Review Committee is a time-consuming process, and there is usually serious competition for such appointments. This means that most members of the HSA have an interest in the health planning process which goes beyond the purely altruistic. The psychiatrist confronting such a committee must be prepared to deal with attitudes and reactions reflecting a variety of hidden agenda. He must be able to respond to them in a tolerant, responsive manner, without provocation.

The consumer who seeks HSA membership may approach a given proposal with a bias related to his constituency's needs or interests, and may present the proposal's supporters with totally unexpected arguments and objections. The psychiatrist may need to discuss a proposed program quite carefully with local officials and community groups in order to assure himself of their support. It is often wise to present letters of support from those governmental bodies and community groups who will be affected by the program. It is equally important to avoid opposition from other health care institutions in the area.

In this dialogue, Dr. Martin mentioned that his hospital has a contract with the county to admit the indigent, chronically ill, and violent patients from the county. A strong letter of endorsement from the county government indicating an urgent need for these new beds might have been enough to obtain approval from the HSA in spite of the unresolved day hospital issue. Institutions experienced in the HSA process will often involve governmental and community groups in the early development of a proposal, and may tailor the proposed program to the needs of these groups in order to assure their support.

In addition to the kind of bias discussed above, HSA consumers will bring to their task a wide range of personal prejudices about health care, its institutions, and especially physicians. Some harbor suspicions that physicians are interested mainly in providing themselves with facilities based not on the public need but on the financial benefits for themselves or their institutions. The psychiatrist must be prepared for the possibility of this anti-physician or anti-hospital prejudice to occur. He must be willing to discuss the financial aspects of the proposal quite openly and especially in relation to physician income. In some HSAs, Dr. Martin's attempt to evade the day hospital issue because of its financial considerations would have created opposition and resentment and might have doomed his proposal.

Some HSA members feel very strongly that health care is too expensive, and subject every proposal to close fiscal scrutiny. They may examine not only the fiscal aspects of the proposal under discussion, but may ask difficult questions about the overall financial status of the sponsoring institutions. Unless the psychiatrist can answer such questions in depth and with confidence, he should bring someone who can do so to any meeting with HSA committees or staff.

The HSA consumer may have all the prejudices about mental illness that are found in the general public, and the psychiatrist must be prepared to deal with them in an educational and non-judgmental manner. He should not be surprised if an advocate of some fringe therapeutic method insists on knowing why this proposal does not include that particular therapy. He must be especially aware of the feelings among many in the public that psychiatrists hospitalize patients unnecessarily or prolong treatment unduly.

Dr. Martin, in this dialogue, did an effective job of explaining why patients may need admission to an inpatient unit. Many community groups are concerned with the problem of deinstitutionalized chronic mental patients living in their neighborhoods. A psychiatrist must be prepared to discuss the impact of his proposal on this problem, and he may encounter criticism if his institution does not treat such patients in its service area. It is essential for the psychiatrist to develop support among the mental health advocacy groups in his area and to involve them in new program development.

The psychiatrist should be aware of other mental health proposals which have come before the review committee, and, if possible, examine other applications before submitting his own. The attitudes of a review committee may have been formed by previous proposals and their advocates. The HSA staff member can inform the psychiatrist of the prevailing attitudes of the review committee toward mental health issues, and may be willing to assist the psychiatrist in dealing with these attitudes in his presentation.

The HSA provider members may present a special set of problems for the psychiatrist. Most of these providers work for hospitals or other institutions, since most independent practitioners cannot afford the financial loss involved in the committee membership. The law specifies the makeup of the provider group, and only a few of them will be physicians. Very few HSAs have psychiatrists as members; in fact, the mental health professions are generally underrepresented. Needless to say, the psychiatrist appearing before an HSA must be aware of the professional orientation and institutional affiliation of all mental health providers. Their attitudes toward his proposal will have a major influence on the committee.

The psychiatrist must be aware of the impact of the proposal on other hospitals or institutions which are represented among the provider members. Since the Health Systems Plan will usually stipulate the maximum number of new beds or other services to be approved in a given area, any institution proposing a new program should first evaluate the plans of neighboring institutions. Open opposition from another hospital will make it very difficult to obtain approval for new beds.

Generally speaking, a psychiatrist who wishes to succeed in an encounter with an HSA must understand the health planning process and the health needs of his area. He must avoid appearing to be a blind advocate of the needs of his institution or profession; instead, he must assume the role of participant in the area's overall health system. His interaction with the HSA should be as partner in the planning process, and he must always avoid assuming an adversary stance.

Point of View: Psychiatry

For many psychiatrists, participation in the health planning process can be a difficult experience. Physicians are frequently shaken by their first contact with groups such as the Health Systems Agency (HSA) which are dominated by citizens. Some discover that their credentials and experience are no protection against critical challenges. Others have difficulty in applying their experience with individual patients to the broader issues of health planning.

Psychiatrists should approach the HSA with a clear understanding of the planning process and the unique problems their professional identity and experience will bring to the process. This dialogue shows how one psychiatrist managed to negotiate this process with partial success, and points out a number of things he did well, as well as several serious errors.

Because he is a physician, the psychiatrist is primarily oriented toward the needs of the individual patients under his care. Even though he had assumed responsibility for the direction of a clinical program, Dr. Martin's primary orientation was for the needs of individual patients. He was concerned about patients who might have committed suicide because of lack of services, about the chronically ill and about violent patients. His principal concern was that his hospital be able to provide services; considerations of cost were secondary.

In order to achieve his primary goal of caring for patients, Dr. Martin proposed the development of expensive inpatient beds. His initial approach to the HSA was to claim that the 20 additional beds are essential, and to avoid any discussion of less costly alternatives such as the day hospital. He either assumed that the HSA committee members do not know enough about the subject to question his claim, or believed that they would accept his statement because he is a knowledgeable professional. Dr. Martin was well equipped with the appropriate statistics and arguments to demonstrate the need for new services; further data showed why his particular institution should receive approval. He mentioned the two suicides to appeal to the humanitarian side of his audience. This type of appeal must be used carefully, since some HSA members may resent being made to feel guilty for ignoring human suffering if they should deny a request for new services. They may be very wary of exaggerated claims of dire need or unrelieved suffering and death. Dr. Martin wisely introduced the subject in an offhand manner which actually led the committee to inquire further about the matter.

Dr. Martin was confronted unexpectedly with a relevant question about the role of day hospital treatment in his proposal and his overall program. He recognized that he was dealing with a knowledgeable questioner, so he discussed the nature of a good day hospital program with the committee. His responses to questions were models of clarity and relevance, which showed his broad knowledge as an administrator and his ability to communicate this knowledge to the educated layman. He avoided using unnecessary professional jargon, which would have confused, bored or irritated committee members.

However, it is obvious that Dr. Martin was avoiding something. From the moment he admitted that he did not have a day hospital program, Dr. Martin lost the initiative in the discussion and was placed in a defensive position. In spite of a second more pointed question about the issue, Dr. Martin again failed to answer directly and openly. Eventually, Dr. Martin had to admit that his Certificate of Need concealed a major issue in cost-effectiveness. He had obviously underestimated the sophistication of the committee members and did not expect such a thorough examination of the issues involved in his proposal. This is one of the most common errors made by psychiatrists, who may feel that a committee of health care consumers will be made up of ordinary citizens who will be impressed with the psychiatrist's medical credentials and will accept his opinions without question. In fact, HSA committees contain many well-informed persons who have been involved in health planning for many years. They are backed up by a paid staff of health planning professionals who research each Certificate of Need application carefully before it reaches the committee level. The psychiatrist appearing before an HSA committee must be very clear about his facts and can expect to be challenged if he is inconsistent. When his professional opinion is requested, he must avoid any attitude of authoritarian condescension, or any attempt to avoid the difficulties in the issue. Dr. Martin may have felt embarrassed to admit that his proposal, and in fact, his entire program, was strongly influenced by financial considerations. It would have been wiser for him to admit this in the beginning rather than to be caught in such an inconsistency.

In this dialogue, Dr. Martin admitted that the most rational proposal for new services would involve a split between inpatient and day hospital beds. He failed to get approval for the 20 beds he requested. The pledge of cooperation between the providers and the HSA to obtain better day hospital reimbursement is an ideal but all-too-rare outcome of this type of situation. The reality is that, even with such a coalition, a change in reimbursement policy will take some time to bring about. In the meantime, Dr. Martin was pressured into the development of a day hospital program as the price of approval of 10 inpatient beds. This is a good example of the process of compromise and negotiation which is an integral part of health planning. Rather than simply pressing the issue, Dr.

Martin showed good judgment in withdrawing his 20-bed proposal. This delay in approval of his bed request plus the likelihood that only half the number of beds requested will be approved may make it difficult for Dr. Martin to provide care for all who need it. The psychiatrist must appreciate and learn to work with this systems approach if he is to succeed in dealing with health planners. The psychiatrist must be careful not to adopt the stance of the righteous "patient advocate" who insists that the needs of his patients must be met whatever the costs. He must also refrain from questioning the motives or judgment of health planners who question his demands.

Discussion

Most of the two preceding commentaries focus on the need to understand the intricacies of an HSA Committee and what happens when a psychiatrist is confronted by a consumer-provider committee that has no psychiatrists as members, but which is required by law to critique and approve (or disapprove) proposals. The psychiatrist should first accept his responsibility to understand thoroughly the origin, need for, and makeup of such committees. The finer points of the hidden agendas, the varying levels of sophistication of the members, and the overall goal and self-image of these committees should be examined prior to contact. Further, this should be done by the psychiatrist keeping in mind the attitudes and politics of the larger community which the HSA is charged by law to represent.

Other issues which should be of interest to the psychiatrist are the methods of evaluation used by those committees and how previous decisions which have an impact on psychiatry were arrived at.

When justified, the psychiatrist must be prepared to challenge with facts the assertions of non-professionals. Nothing less will do. Any hint of condescension or less than a complete and honest disclosure in response to appropriate concerns expressed by the committee members will show up any inherent bias that exists within the committee when a professional attempts to present a proposal. This concern requires an awareness that any flaws and weaknesses of one's proposal should be discussed up front. Doing so will add strength to the presentation and to the psychiatrist's credibility, reducing the potential for confrontation and rejection of the proposal. Acceptance of a valid criticism that was not foreseen and the ability to field it intelligently and expertly will also provide an opportunity to increase the committee's confidence in the psychiatrist and in his proposal.

Citizen dominated committees, as represented by HSAs, must also recognize that professions, including psychiatry, are not yet accustomed to the new requirements which mandate external review by non-professionals and reduce their previous authority to act independently. Therefore, HSAs have the responsibility to educate psychiatrists and other professionals on the process and content of their procedures, while, at the same time, engaging in a continued self-examination which will protect against the emergence of an anti-professional bias. An awareness of these responsibilities by both parties to the dialogue and a mutual acknowledgment of their appropriateness, when carried out properly, is essential if confrontation is to be reduced.

The administrative psychiatrist's awareness of costs and other economic realities is important not only in his attempts to obtain new resources through the local health planning process, but also in his attempts to obtain support through appropriations as illustrated in the Interface on the budget analyst.

7

**INTERFACE VI
THE BUDGET ANALYST**

Acknowledgments

We gratefully acknowledge the assistance of the following in the preparation of this chapter:

William S. Allerton, *Eagleville State Hospital, Eagleville PA*

James Bateman, *Joint Legislative Budget Committee, State of Arizona, Phoenix AZ*

James W. Bibb, *Director of the Budget, State of Kansas Department of Administration, Topeka KS*

William Goldman, *Medical Director, Rockridge Health Care Plan, Oakland, California; Former Director of Mental Health for the City and County of San Francisco, San Francisco CA*

Charles P. McIntosh, *Former Budget Secretary, Governor's Budget Office, Commonwealth of Pennsylvania, Harrisburg PA*

Bryce Hughett, *Executive Director, Area 3 Mental Health Center, Billings MT*

7

Interface VI

The Budget Analyst

DIALOGUE

SETTING: The following dialogue takes place in the office of a community mental health center director who is being visited by a member of the Governor's Budget Office Staff. This center receives part of its budget from legislatively appropriated funds. The specific purpose of the staff member's visit is to review concerns about State funding for community mental health programs. The Budget Officer also informs the mental health center director about issues which should be addressed in the upcoming budget proposal to the State.

PARTICIPANTS: Mr. Walter Cochran: Staff member, Executive Budget Office, Office of the Governor.
Dr. William Morris: A psychiatrist who is director of a community mental health center.

Mr. Cochran: Before we get started, Bill, I think you should understand the Executive Budget Office's role in funding requests. A Budget Analyst makes recommendations that go to the Governor's office where the final budgeting decision for your program is made. If funding for mental health services is high in priority, these programs will be more likely to get the amount of money requested. Our recommendations don't necessarily continue throughout the budgetary process.

I've got several questions about your request for next year but I'm not sure that they are in any kind of order. For example, could you tell me who determines the level of funding for your different programs, such as screening and evaluation, prevention and education?

Dr. Morris: That's determined in several different ways. The program is operated, under my direction, with the assistance of an Executive Council. The Council consists of the directors of the major divisions: Adult Pre-Care, which includes screening and evaluation; Adult Outpatient; Child Care; Day Treatment; Halfway House; and what we call Treatment Support Services which include prevention services, research and evaluation services, and other support services.

We assess our needs in terms of each of those divisions. They also serve as our cost centers. If, in the course of our budget planning, we see a need in one of these areas, it is the responsibility of the manager of that area to document that need and to present it to me and to the Executive Council. He or she evaluates the level of services required based upon utilization and other data.

In our budgetary planning process, all these needs are presented to the Executive Council for review and recommendations. I set the priorities and forward the budget to the State for its review.

Mr. Cochran: That's about the way it's done in most centers. But tell me, have you seen the comprehensive model delivery system that the community mental health agencies have been putting together?

Dr. Morris: Yes. We participated in the process that led to the package. I've studied the final product, and find that I like it quite a bit. It tries to describe, for a given population, the types and levels of services required.

In terms of the population we serve, it would be fair to say that our current level of services, in comparison to that described in the model we have available, is under their recommended levels.

Mr. Cochran: Explain to me how you came to that conclusion. How do you determine who gets the service? Is it the ability to pay, the severity of the disease, or what? Is there an attempt to measure the effectiveness of existing programs?

Dr. Morris: Well, as you know, our mandate is to serve people regardless of their ability to pay. This is true for all three mental health centers in our community. We're required by the State and Federal governments to have a sliding fee scale. The top of the scale is determined by the cost per unit of each type of service provided. This cost is adjusted downward according to income and other considerations through the fee schedule. Consequently, some may receive free services. The sliding fee scale is updated every year, and is based upon new cost data.

Mr. Cochran: Are you satisfied that your administrative people follow up on the patient's ability to pay? Are you satisfied that people who really are able to pay are paying? And then the last part of my question—my original three questions—are you trying to measure the effectiveness of your existing programs?

Dr. Morris: Walt, in response to your first question, my answer is no. I am not satisfied. I think we could do a better job of collecting funds for the services we render. On the other hand, I think we are doing a better job than we were a year or two ago.

One of the administrative steps we have taken is to centralize, to a certain extent, our fee collection mechanism. On the other hand, we feel that fees and the determination of fees are, in many ways, an issue in therapy. Consequently, we leave it to our therapists to make the initial evaluation with regard to what fee the person ought to be paying. Those data are provided on a card which is then forwarded to me.

Mr. Cochran: How do you know if people are telling you the truth?

Dr. Morris: We don't. We have absolutely no mechanism to check the accuracy of data that people give us and that's an obvious weakness.

On the other hand, if you look statistically at the population we serve, I don't think you will find much difference between what people tell us they make and what we assume they make. Would it be worthwhile to do more checks; to employ people for this purpose? Would the financial return warrant that additional cost? My answer is, "I don't think so."

Of the fees that are billed, the collection rate is quite high, but the overall amount of fees billed is not as high as I would like, or as high as I think it could be. It has been going up over the last few years, and I hope it will continue to go up.

Mr. Cochran: How about third-party claims? How are you doing with those?

Dr. Morris: Again, for those people who have third-party reimbursement mechanisms, we are doing pretty well. We do have one interesting problem which I would like to share with you. A person will come here who has third-party coverage with both a deductible and a co-insurance requirement; but from their own cash resources, they can't meet the deductible or the co-insurance. We then have many problems justifying to the insurance company our right to collect the third-party reimbursement.

Mr. Cochran: In some of the statistics we have, we have noticed that administrative costs of community mental health agencies in this state range anywhere from 7 to 32 percent. We have to conclude that either the monitoring system of the State or the efforts of agencies to control administrative costs isn't fully adequate.

Dr. Morris: That's an awfully wide range, and the truth, for us, is roughly in the middle. I can give you an approximate breakdown of our administrative costs and what they include. Approximately 20 percent of our costs are "direct" administrative costs.

Mr. Cochran: We think the State should have some influence on the administrative costs of the community mental health centers. Don't you agree?

Dr. Morris: I believe so. When a proposal from an agency goes to the State for State funds, we are requesting the State to undertake a certain portion of the cost of that program. Because of that, I would agree that the State does have a responsibility to monitor the entire program.

Mr. Cochran: Would you say that the State's monitoring of services and expenditures is effective?

Dr. Morris: My personal judgment is that it is fairly effective. But what may not be adequate are the guidelines which you provide for assessing these costs.

For example, a lot depends on how you define administrative costs. Different organizations tend to define their administrative costs differently. There should be clear guidelines as to what administrative costs are before these percentages are computed.

For example, when we have a secretary working in our Adult Outpatient Services in support of the clinical services being provided in that area, we don't call that an administrative cost. We call it part of the cost of providing Adult Outpatient Services; without the secretarial component, there is no way that the staff would be able to see patients, make notes, and keep records which are part of the clinical care. Other agencies probably do it differently.

Mr. Cochran: I see your point but that's not how we look at it. We definitely define such secretarial work as administrative costs. I imagine if you counted that and some other things, it would drive your administrative percentage way up.

Dr. Morris: It certainly would. If you defined administrative costs in the broadest possible way and got everybody to adhere to the same definition, I wouldn't be surprised if you found that the administrative budget of this place, or *any* of the other community mental health programs, would reach 40 to 50 percent.

I think, however, that you need to consider some other things. If our total budget, including administrative costs, is allocated to the direct service programs, the cost per hour of service is low. For example, in our Adult Outpatient Service, the cost is $32 an hour. That is certainly less than the cost of a similar service in the private psychiatric and psychological sectors. Even if 40 percent of that $32 an hour is an "administrative cost," the total program is still more cost-effective than the private sector.

In addition, you should remember that our operation is a multi-service approach; services pre-delivered within a system rather than via an independent practitioner. So, these administrative costs, I think, are justifiable.

Mr. Cochran: Now we're getting into the area of competitiveness. When you said the $32 was cheaper than in the private sector, what did you mean?

Dr. Morris: The part of the private sector I'm referring to is the independent private practitioner in the community. The cost per hour of service, as I understand it, among the three community mental health agencies here is in the vicinity of $32 to

$36 an hour. This is less than the cost of a private psychiatric practitioner who charges an average of $50 to $60 an hour.

Mr. Cochran: Can we get back to that model comprehensive system we talked about a few minutes ago? Were you satisfied with its optimal levels of service in those eighteen different areas?

Dr. Morris: I think that those service requirements of the model comprehensive system, as described in the package presented to you and to the Legislature this past year, were generally acceptable. I think it does a good job in terms of outlining an optimal system. I think the package tells you how we want to go about building a system. I don't think anybody feels that such a system should be built overnight. There are parts of that system that have a greater priority.

Mr. Cochran: I know what you mean. I sort of felt that we ought to take the ten most important out of the eighteen and build those to a 90 percent level, for example, before tackling the last eight. But my understanding from the program people in the State mental health office is that they want to spread the money across all eighteen, and that they would rather have eighteen areas funded at the 50 percent level rather than ten at 100 percent.

Dr. Morris: Well, part of the reason for that might be Federal requirements. As I indicated to you, many of the community mental health programs have Federal funds, and those Federal funds have service requirements which are included within the eighteen that were described. Therefore, part of the reason for the State Office's decision may be that compliance in each of those eighteen areas at some level, runs less risk of losing Federal funds.

Mr. Cochran: Did you say earlier that when you compared your delivery level to those norms or goals, that you were beneath them in most areas?

Dr. Morris: Yes. In my opinion, we're beneath them in terms of what you might expect as the optimal level of service for the number of people in this particular area.

In terms of the eighteen services, our major weakness is probably in the specialized service areas. For example, we only have one Halfway House Program for the 450,000 people in this county and no children's residential mental health programs.

Mr. Cochran: That brings up another question I wanted to ask. How effective is your Halfway House Program? The fact of the matter is that there are only so many dollars available to support behavioral health programs. Regardless of the mechanics of the funding, local mental health agencies have indicated a willingness to be judged on a number of points. One is cost-effectiveness which we have talked about briefly. Another is whether the need exists and I don't think really anybody can argue about that at this low level of funding.

The thing that concerns me most is how effective these programs are. What have you been doing in this area to demonstrate the effectiveness of the programs?

Dr. Morris: Well, I appreciate your concern because it's an area that I've been trying to generate some concern in for a long time.

Now you ask an interesting question about our Halfway House. There we have a unique problem because many of the people leave the Halfway House, but are not yet ready to move toward independent living in the community. We have an acute shortage in this community of intermediate types of living arrangements.

One of the things we are proposing to the State for next year is an apartment program. We propose to subsidize apartments, to a limited extent. People would then be paying rent back to us and the apartments would serve as a transition from our Halfway House to an independent living situation.

The data indicate (and we concur) that if this program were available, the rate of recidivism would go down. People who come out of our Halfway House Program and go into the community have a fairly high rate of recidivism in relation to treatment. One of the reasons is that it's too big a jump from the Halfway House to independent community living.

That's one example of the kind of planning, based upon evaluation, we are trying to do.

Mr. Cochran: Tell us about the impact that you've made on the number of patients going to the State Hospital. If additional funds were made available, how many patients at the State Hospital could return here?

Dr. Morris: That's particularly difficult to quantify because I believe that our impact has been on keeping patients out in the first place. Over the last four to five years, the level of patients at the State Hospital from our county has remained relatively consistent—between 65 to 75. You should keep in mind that roughly 40 percent of that number are either mentally retarded or are individuals in the Maximum Security Section with criminal charges.

We have one of the lowest state hospital utilization rates of any of the counties within the State.

Our goal over the last few years has been to maintain that rate. We don't think that we could or should ever abolish utilization of the State Hospital. We don't think that would be appropriate or cost-effective because there are people who do require that kind of care and it's not effective to develop it at the local level.

On the other hand, we are seriously concerned that if we can't maintain the current level of services in the community, the eventual result is going to be that the number using the State Hospital is going to go up.

We think it can be avoided only if there is adequate funding for community-based services. We believe that the future direction for the State should be a primary investment in community-based mental health services as a way of avoiding the higher cost of investing in inpatient services, not to mention the human cost to people who require that kind of institutionalization.

Mr. Cochran: Well, Doctor, I think that it would be interesting for you to know the approach that the Executive Budget Office and the Governor are going to take this year toward your budget. The Budget Office is going to work in teams with the Department of Economic Planning and Development which is part of the Governor's Office. We'll have planners and auditor-type people as well as budget analysts who will be looking into your existing programs, and attempting to identify whether we're getting a dollar's worth of service out of the dollar the Legislature has appropriated for you. We'll also be looking at all the new projects that you're proposing to the State for support, the dollar amounts, and the feasibility.

We're going to be asking you to identify at least 20 percent of your current base and to provide policy statements. These policy statements will consist of identifying the relevant issues in that 20 percent of the base: the problems, the goals, and the objectives. These will be used in examining your new requests. We'll ask you to give us several viable alternatives and the cost/benefits of your programs.

Dr. Morris: I certainly welcome that. I think that any organization such as ours that receives State tax dollars wants to be able to communicate the justifications for those needs.

Mr. Cochran: Just as a parting shot—when people have the money, they probably end up in the private sector and not at the

The Budget Analyst 131

community mental health sector, don't they? If a member of your family was in need of one of your services, would you have any reservations about them being treated here?

Dr. Morris: No. I would have absolutely no compunction about them receiving care here. However, my response is probably different from what you would get from the general public who, if they have the dollars available, tend to feel that, for those dollars, it is their prerogative to select a particular practitioner. This is, of course, not the prerogative of the individual who comes here because we rotate intake. In many instances, the general public chooses to go only to a psychiatrist.

Mr. Cochran: Thank you very much.

Point of View: Budget Officer

Non-psychiatric commentators described the dialogue as typical (or "all too common"). They criticized both Mr. Cochran and Dr. Morris for dwelling on the secondary issues of efficient program management, while neglecting the primary issue of program effectiveness. As one commentator put it, "The level of the dialogue is on a plane that might interest an agency comptroller or an agency budget analyst, but it does not seem to be the approach desired by the Governor's Budget Officer. The budget process is designed to determine the need or demand for services and the effect that such services have on individuals, institutions and the environment. Once it is determined that there is a need or demand for a program and that government intervention may have a beneficial effect, then questions of efficiency, alternative approaches to problems and least cost methods can be sensibly addressed." According to this view, the Budget Officer's primary goal is to determine this community's need for mental health services, and to obtain evidence of what impact Dr. Morris's service system has on that need. This information will provide the basis for his recommendations to the Governor concerning funding priorities. Dr. Morris's goal is, therefore, to convince Mr. Cochran of the reality of the need, of the effectiveness of his CMHC in addressing it, and to provide him with solid evidence with which to convince others.

Mr. Cochran can be criticized for asking unfocused questions and for accepting vague answers. For example, his first question, "Who determines the level of funding for your different programs?" was thought to be less useful than "What criteria are used to determine levels of funding?" Dr. Morris's answer provided no information that the budget analyst can use to judge the appropriateness of the levels requested, but he did not press the point. Much of the dialogue is devoted to details of program administration such as fee assessment and collection and the definition of "administrative cost." When Mr. Cochran finally asked what seemed to them to be a key question, "What have you been doing in this area to prove effectiveness of programs?" Dr. Morris responded by alluding to, but not producing, data that would prove effectiveness. Mr. Cochran did not press Dr. Morris for these data. The dialogue could just as easily have taken place in the 50's with the superintendent of a mental hospital. Central offices are still asking the same questions and psychiatrists are still responding with the same answers. The development of cost centers, accounting methods, and workload data are only part of the problem. The significant part remains unanswered, and that is the real effect of such programs on the mental health of our people.

One final point, drawn more from the tone of the commentaries, should be made. While both Mr. Cochran and Dr. Morris were regarded as rather muddle-headed, there were some hints that Dr. Morris was also seen as evasive. This is expressed by observations such as, "The doctor ignores the question about program effectiveness." By not perceiving and responding to the fundamental concerns of the Budget Officer, Dr. Morris seemed to have given the impression that he has something to hide. In this way, attitudes may develop which complicate communication, and which may generalize. The commentator quoted above went on to note, "This is typical of persons in the mental health field."

Point of View: Psychiatry

The psychiatrists who commented on the dialogue stressed the importance of a thorough exploration of the context of the interaction to the facilitation of communication. It is important to understand the biases that each participant brought to the discussion, and to understand the structure and functioning of the organizations in which they work. One commentator noted, "This case study also presumes a uniform kind of government and state structure even though there are fifty of them (no two the same) which change a minimum of once every four years!"

It is important for mental health administrators to use encounters such as this to educate and persuade government officials. One reviewer suggests that, "Many budget officers ... are actually unaware of the high percentages of funding that have gone to mental health programs ... millions of dollars have been poured into mental health programs ... with little or no attempt at accountability."

A strong caution was stated in the use of private practice fees as a justification for cost effectiveness of CMHC outpatient services. Many patient contacts in CMHCs are not by psychiatrists and the private fees of non-psychiatrists are more competitive. CMHC fees should stand on their own merit, including the mainly indirect services performed, the organizational costs for continuing care, and others.

As Mr. Cochran began to probe issues such as the Center's budget process and fee collections, Dr. Morris responded with generalities unsupported by facts. This might appear to be a rather patronizing attitude, which implies, "we are taking care of it and we know best", without deigning to provide the data upon which his conclusion rests.

The multiplicity of standards imposed on mental health agencies by accrediting, certifying, and funding agencies often produce chaos in our evaluative attempts. What has not been developed to date, to a sufficient degree, are appropriate process and output standards. This should not force the mental health administrator to adopt a defensive posture, however. Mental health professionals have been made so aware of being regarded as dealing in "ephemeral matters" that they have overcompensated. The fact is that they are frequently held accountable far in excess of requirements in other areas in federal, state, and local governmets.

Discussion

A theme that runs through the commentaries is the need for clear questions, direct answers, and careful consideration of all of the relevant supporting data. The vagueness in the discussion, which included carelessly phrased questions, wandering replies and a lack of follow-up, was very troublesome. It is essential that both parties be clear about their objectives, and that these goals be pursued in a logical way.

The meeting described in this dialogue must have been initiated by the Budget Officer because he asked most of the questions. A budget official in such a situation has two types of concerns: first, to assess the impact of the service programs on the mental health of the community (program effectiveness); and second, to assess the quality of the program's management (program efficiency). Logically, the first comes before the second. The Governor's task is to determine whether money spent on community mental health is money well-spent.

The Budget Analyst 135

It would be wise for the program director to draw out an explicit statement of these objectives at the outset of the interview, if possible. Mr. Cochran's opening statement was undoubtedly accurate, but gave no clue as to the specific issues that he planned to address. His admission that he is not sure his questions are "in any kind of order" suggests that he is either disorganized or crafty. In such circumstances the interviewee should attempt to create some structure for the interview.

The basic concern of the administrator, at this time of the year, is to present a persuasive justification for the Center's budget requests. A meeting such as this provides a valuable opportunity to try out his arguments and to develop an alliance with the Budget Officer. Thus, Dr. Morris needed to educate as he answered, and to solicit reactions, comments and advice from his audience.

The director should respond to the Budget Officer's questions by laying out the logic of the decisions, as well as the information used. A focus on this sort of response will help keep one from being misled by a poorly phrased question. For example, when Mr. Cochran asked, "Who determines the levels of funding?", Dr. Morris should have answered the question but then continued on to the "how" question that should be behind it. It is then a natural step to provide the relevant data that led to this year's budgetary decisions. In this way, Dr. Morris could have begun to build his case and to assess its strengths and weaknesses in Mr. Cochran's eyes.

In all discussions about budgets, the director should rely on his fiscal officer for data, and, when appropriate, should invite him to the meeting.

By presenting the logic of the budgeting process, the director can also introduce the Budget Officer to the constraints to which the Center is subject (very few of which come from the

Budget Office). These constraints have considerable relevance to the question of program effectiveness, inasmuch as they reflect the body of accumulated wisdom about what constitutes good (effective) clinical and administrative practice. In the absence of hard research data proving that certain methods are effective in reducing the incidence of mental disorder, evidence that services provided are the most effective may have to do.

This, then, brings us to the question of evaluation or outcome research, the sore spot that accounts for a good deal of the communication problem between clinicians and administrators. If Dr. Morris appeared evasive as well as dull-witted to one of the non-psychiatric commentators, it was probably because he seemed to be avoiding this issue. It must be faced squarely.

One point that needs to be made is that because something is difficult to measure doesn't necessarily mean it is unreal. Every opportunity must be taken to explain the difficulties and accomplishments of evaluation research, and to provide all of the pertinent evidence available. It is equally important, as one of the psychiatric commentators suggested, to compare the evidence for the effectiveness of mental health interventions with those of other human services fields.

Requests for and concerns about measures of treatment effectiveness are by no means limited to administrators. They trouble legislators also at the Federal as well as the State level, as the Interface on the legislator illustrates.

8

**INTERFACE VII
THE LEGISLATOR**

Acknowledgments

We gratefully acknowledge the assistance of the following in the preparation of this chapter:

Peter G. Bourne, *Coordinator, U.N. International Drinking Water Supply and Sanitation Decade; Former Special Assistant to the President for Health Issues, Washington DC*

Robert J. Campbell, *Medical Director, Gracie Square Hospital, New York NY*

Jay Cutler, *Director, Department of Governmental Relations, American Psychiatric Association, Washington DC*

Stanley B. Jones, *Partner, Fullerton, Jones and Wolkstein, Health Policy Alternatives, Incorporated, Silver Spring, Maryland; Former Staff Member, Senate Health Subcommittee, Washington DC*

Gerald L. Klerman, *Former Administrator, Alcohol, Drug Abuse, and Mental Health Administration, Rockville MD*

Robert M. Smucker, *Vice President for Government Relations for Independent Sector, Washington DC; Former National Program Director, The National Mental Health Association, Rosslyn, VA*

8

Interface VII

The Legislator

DIALOGUE

SETTING: The following dialogue takes place in a hearing room of the United States Senate. A psychiatrist, who represents a national mental health organization concerned with community mental health services, has been invited to appear before a Senate Subcommittee to discuss the Federal effort in mental health and to respond to questions from the Subcommittee regarding congressional concerns about that effort.

PARTICIPANTS: Senator Powers: Member, Senate Subcommittee
Senator James: Member, Senate Subcommittee
Senator Alpert: Member, Senate Subcommittee
Dr. Dodd: A psychiatrist and director of a national mental health organization

Senator Powers: In the formation of the community mental health center concept, Congress was talking about treatment of severe mental illness in the community. How do you reconcile this objective with the lack of attention to treatment of seriously mentally ill patients in many community mental health programs?

Dr. Dodd: I would agree that there are many community health programs that have not been sufficiently diligent in orienting their services toward the more severely mentally ill.

However, I think it is important to recognize that, in many instances, alternative resources may not be available for people with less severe forms of mental illness. Consequently, in these communities, the center is viewed as the *only* resource for the care they require, even if the individual is not among the more seriously mentally ill. While mental health programs should give priority attention to the needs of the seriously mentally ill, I would suggest that this not be done by limiting the ability of the centers to provide care and treatment to less seriously ill persons.

Senator Alpert: The President's Commission on Mental Health calls for a broader range of services to persons with chronic mental illness. From my reading of the report, many of those services aren't mental health services. Why should we pay for them from mental health funding?

Dr. Dodd: I would agree with you that those services should not necessarily be funded out of mental health resources. However, many programs have had to fund those services out of mental health resources because of the lack of availability, for example, of appropriate social service funding to support the cost of these services.

Title XX, which is the primary Federal social services funding mechanism, has been available only to meet the needs of the mentally ill in the most limited way. Many state Title XX authorities assume that since these people are mentally ill, all of their services should come under the mental health umbrella and be funded from mental health resources.

Senator James: We've now opened up what appears to be a Pandora's box of the distinction between mental illness services and mental health/human services. I understand the need for the latter in conjunction with, and in support of, the former. The question I now present to you is whether, in view of this mixed bag of health and social services which many mentally ill patients need, a psychiatrist should be the chief professional person on board and the administrator of each community mental health center?

Dr. Dodd: I believe that every community mental health center should have psychiatric direction to the clinical portion of its programs. That's not the same as saying that the psychiatrist needs to be the overall administrator of the center. Frankly, there are probably not enough psychiatrists who are adequately trained in administration to handle that aspect of a community mental health organization.

Senator James: Therefore, you feel that there must be at least some sort of contractual arrangement with a community or local psychiatrist by the community mental health center?

Dr. Dodd: I would go further than that. I would say that the requirements should be for the direct employment of a psychiatrist unless there are circumstances that militate against this possibility despite the good faith efforts of the community mental health program.

Senator Powers: If we had that requirement and an adequate number of psychiatrists were not available, what role would the psychiatrist play?

Dr. Dodd: I would suggest that each community mental health center be required to develop policies which clearly detail the role of the psychiatrist in the initial assessment process. This would ensure that there is psychiatric input into the decision-making process which would determine the nature of treatment. Therefore, it would be clear how the psychiatrist has been involved in the assessment, and what his supervisory role is, regardless of who actually delivers the treatment.

Senator Powers: That answer leads me to the conclusion that a substantial proportion of the patients seen by community mental health centers may not need the services of a psychiatrist. Is this correct?

Dr. Dodd: I think that's an accurate statement because, in my own view, psychiatric practitioners have skills that are superior to the skills of other mental health professionals in certain areas such as diagnosis and evaluation, and the development of treatment plans. Yet, the actual delivery of the therapeutic services, particularly if there is no medication involved, does not necessarily have to be provided by a psychiatrist.

Senator James: It seems to me that such a process would just make the cost of evaluation and treatment very expensive. If a psychiatrist has to be in charge and is receiving a fee for his overview of the services, the cost of treatment will really add up.

Dr. Dodd: It really depends on the nature of the services the psychiatrist provides. If the psychiatrist's role in providing input into the diagnostic and treatment planning process brings him into actual face-to-face contact with the patient, then a separate fee would seem justified.

On the other hand, if the role of psychiatrists is to review the diagnostic assessment data and to provide input to the treatment plan in conjunction with another non-medical mental health professional, a separate fee would not seem to be justified. The cost of these services could be incorporated into the general service fee which is set by the program.

Senator Powers: Should a psychiatrist participate in such a program if he has not had a face-to-face meeting with the patient, at least one or more times, when chemotherapy is a part of the treatment plan?

The Legislator 143

Dr. Dodd: No, I'm not suggesting that the psychiatrist should only be a supervisor. If chemotherapy is a part of the treatment plan, then that treatment must be delivered by the psychiatrist.

Senator Alpert: Let's talk about some of the specialized requirements for centers. One of these is the tie-in to deinstitutionalization. It appears, from looking at the data available, that the community mental health center has, in great measure, not met its obligation vis-á-vis the deinstitutionalized patient. What recommendations, if any, do you have to tighten that tie?

Dr. Dodd: Well, I agree with your conclusion, but I do not think the responsibility lies only with the community mental health center. In many ways, I feel the community mental health center has been a victim of forces beyond its control. Let me give you some illustrations.

The entire question of community housing for the deinstitutionalized patient has been a neglected area, both at the Federal and State levels. It has been extremely difficult to utilize housing dollars for the development of housing services to deinstitutionalized patients. When appropriate housing services are not available, it becomes very difficult for the community mental health program to deliver effective services to the deinstitutionalized patient.

Also, as I mentioned earlier, many deinstitutionalized patients require, in addition to mental health treatment services, appropriate social services. When the center has attempted to take a leadership role in the provision of those social services, it has found the going rough because it receives criticism from two different directions—from those in the mental health field who feel it is not within the purview of community mental health programs to be delivering social services, and from those in the social service field who believe that mental health programs should be delivering mental health services and not social services. The end result is that funding for social services to these deinstitutionalized patients is not provided.

Senator James: If a mental health center makes a determination that there are no housing services available to the person who is about to become deinstitutionalized, would you support some override that would require that patient to remain in an institution rather than leave it at that point?

Dr. Dodd: I don't think that's the solution. First, I think there could be some serious legal questions raised in the case of the voluntarily admitted individual or the involuntarily committed patient who is no longer dangerous to self or others.

Frankly, I think the only solution is to increase everyone's awareness of this problem and to make certain that other funding resources, such as housing and social services, give adequate recognition to the needs of this population.

Senator James: Let's turn, if we might, to another specialized group, the elderly. Our data indicate a lack of adequate performance by community mental health centers on behalf of the elderly. What do you think could be done in future legislation to ensure better services for the elderly?

Dr. Dodd: Well, again, I think your observation is correct, but I believe that the reason for this underutilization of services in community mental health programs by the elderly is much more complex than is generally recognized.

First, I think it is important to point out that the stigma associated with going to a mental health program is particularly high among the elderly. A strong mental health program for the elderly must have a strong prevention-oriented focus, with multiple outreach efforts that go into the community and reach the elderly in their natural settings.

The bind in which many mental health programs find themselves is that not enough categorical funding is available for these purposes. Reimbursement is not available to the center for these services because they are not viewed as "traditional" mental health services.

One appropriate Federal response to this problem would be to ensure the continuance of categorical funding for the development of strong prevention and education programs which are to be directed to the elderly.

Senator James: Would it be fair to assume the same response with respect to children?

Dr. Dodd: I think the problem is similar. However, there is a tremendous shortage of personnel who are trained in the care and treatment of children. The difficulty that many mental health programs have in providing adequate services to children, as with the elderly, is finding individuals who are skilled in providing these services.

Senator Alpert: One of the difficulties I see is that the main thrust of Congress, vis-a-vis community mental health centers; that is, national health insurance ultimately will alleviate the need for a categorical funding mechanism. At the same time, under national health insurance the services you have mentioned that are not "medical" would probably not be reimbursed.

How do you reconcile these concepts, or do you believe that a categorical program will have to continue?

Dr. Dodd: I think, as my last answer was trying to indicate, that regardless of what occurs with the development of third-party reimbursements for mental illness, whether through the private sector or a national health insurance program, some types of categorical funding for mental health will need to continue if the broad array of services that are mandated are to be made available and all people are to be reached.

Senator Powers: Now, let me ask the one question that is the basis for many of our concerns about community mental health centers and all mental health treatment. Have you reviewed the effectiveness of treatment? What are your criteria to determine whether or not the patients you see have been effectively treated?

Dr. Dodd: We feel strongly committed to the development of protocols which will allow us to do adequate outcome assessment. At the same time, we recognize that this is a complex issue. Factors which influence outcome go far beyond the efficacy of the treatment delivered.

At the present time, the measures we use to assess effectiveness of treatment are primarily rehospitalization data, frequency of contact, frequency of return to the mental health program and length of stay in treatment. Subjective and objective measurements of perceived improvement which are obtained from both the patient and the therapist during and after treatment are also important.

We are strongly committed to developing other measures. However, I must point out that their development will add to the cost of treatment. At present, the only way to pay for developing sophisticated measurements is by adding to the cost of the treatment service, unless categorical funding is made available for these purposes.

Senator Alpert: As you know, with respect to community mental health centers, we have always made provision for NIMH or the Secretary to authorize evaluations. To your knowledge, are there any definitive evaluations which demonstrate that the services have been effective?

Dr. Dodd: While your initial statement is technically correct, Senator, the present law requires a community mental health center to use a percentage of the funds available to it for evaluation purposes. As a result, no additional funds are made available by the Secretary, or through legislation, for this purpose. It is an example of another of the many requirements placed upon community mental health centers without additional funding.

There have been some projects funded through the demonstration research project component of the NIMH regarding treatment effectiveness of mental health programs and I certainly can provide you and members of the Committee with a list of those studies at a later date.

Senator Alpert: That would be most helpful. To your knowledge, are there any definitive evaluation studies contained in the material you will submit to the Committee?

Dr. Dodd: Well, again, I am not certain what you mean by "definitive," but we will certainly provide to the Committee the work of many individuals, both in the field of psychiatry and other disciplines, who have evaluated the effectiveness of community mental health programs and mental health treatment. There are studies which assess the effectiveness of community mental health programs relative to state hospital utilization, to symptom improvement, to increased level of functioning, etc.

Senator Powers: One might read the President's Commission as saying that the time has come to move away from a goal of a complete network of comprehensive community mental health centers throughout the nation. Would you agree with that conclusion?

Dr. Dodd: Yes, I would agree with that conclusion, insofar as the Commission was urging the continuing availability of funding for the development of a system of community mental health services throughout the country. The Commission points out that the model of a community mental health center may not be the most appropriate or cost-effective mechanism for the development of the system in areas where centers do not already exist. Better linkages between the private and the public sector may be another route for the development of these systems of services.

Senator Powers: Will you share with the Committee your views on how it could modify existing law to strengthen and improve the Community Mental Health Centers Act with respect to cost-effectiveness and quality of services effectiveness?

Dr. Dodd: I think there are a number of things that the Committee could look at in revising existing legislation.

First, there is a great need to tie the planning mechanisms which exist in the Community Mental Health Centers Act and the National Health Planning and Resource Development Act to service delivery strategies. Before further consideration of funding for additional community mental health services is considered, each service area within a state should have a plan available which can be used in the assessment of what is required. Such a plan should take into account all of the resources in the community and not just simply the resources that are provided by publicly supported programs such as community mental health centers. This will enable the Federal Government to better allocate the limited dollars available for new services and to allow communities to build networks of services incrementally.

Second, I think that there is a need to revise existing financing legislation, principally Medicaid and Medicare, so it is more flexible with regard to availability of third-party resources for mental health care.

Finally, I refer again to one of my earlier points. If Congress intends to continue to foster the development of a broad range of services within the framework of a service system, it will have to recognize that there are certain services which won't, and should not be, reimbursed through third-party health care payment. Yet, services that fall into this category, such as

The Legislator

prevention and outreach, are essential to a comprehensive service system. Provision for continued categorical funding of these services on an indefinite basis will have to be made.

Senator Powers: One final question. The community mental health centers concept was developed in an era when doing good for mankind without consideration of fiscal limitations was the mood on a national or state level. Now we've moved into an era of fiscal priorities and limited resources. Do you have any recommendations for prioritizing who should receive services and what services should be provided?

Dr. Dodd: I think the problem here involves creation of definitions of a comprehensive network, and increased flexibility as to how that goal is to be reached.

With regard to who should receive services, I think that basically it would be fair to give the more seriously mentally ill priority over the less seriously mentally ill.

Senator Alpert: I'd like to have your response on one final concern. In DSM III,* as I understand it, smoking is considered a "disorder." We have no data on the efficacy of treatment for smoking. The need to cut back on smoking is serious, but is there any evidence that psychiatry or any of the mental health disciplines have been successful in persuading people to cut back on smoking?

Dr. Dodd: Well, I am not expert enough to answer that specific question. But what your question raises is the more critical issue as to whether, under a national health insurance program, community mental health programs and independent practitioners would be reimbursed for providing "mental health services" to individuals who are defined as having smoking disorders.

---

* American Psychiatric Association, *Diagnostic and Statistical Manual of Mental Disorders*, third edition.

That is not a decision for me to make. That is a decision for the Congress when it sets the framework of its community mental health center and national health insurance legislation. If there is recognition that mental health care is a part of health care and properly should be included within a health-care reimbursement mechanism, whether categorical or non-categorical, guidelines regarding the limits of what can be paid for, in my view, would be relatively acceptable to both community mental health centers and independent practitioners.

Senator Alpert: So what you are saying is that you see no problem with respect to the psychiatrist's Diagnostic Manual including smoking as a disorder on the same grounds, for example, that surgeons include cosmetic surgery? It's just a decision on what is to be reimbursed.

Dr. Dodd: Well, in the same way that the legal definition of insanity is a legal definition and not a medical term, there can be a set of medical diagnostic criteria as are included in DSM III, but it doesn't necessarily have to be the same definition that is used by a legislative body in determining what will be reimbursed.

Senator Powers: Thank you very much.

Point of View: Non-Mental Health Decision-Maker

The non-psychiatrists who commented on this dialogue concurred that Dr. Dodd, while presenting interesting and informative material at the Senate hearing, missed several opportunities to make important and telling points. This was due, in part, to his lack of focus and apparent lack of familiarity with the underlying political issues inherent in a public hearing. The recommendations and criticisms offered by the non-medical professionals provide psychiatrists with concrete strategies to make the most of their contact with government legislators. In making a presentation, psychiatrists must consider the nature of the forum, the expectations of the legislators, the needs of their districts and the best way to focus their material so that key points are conveyed.

Open Senate hearings are not the only forum available to the psychiatrist who is interested in addressing the legislature and affecting legislation. The "real" decision-making and influencing often take place prior to the actual testimony, and are determined, to a large extent, by the information and recommendations gathered by legislative (e.g., Senate) aides. If the goal of the psychiatrist is to shape the voting pattern, an informal meeting with key staff far enough in advance of the vote date may be productive. Nonetheless, the public hearing has the advantage of getting the case on the record, which in itself has several ramifications.

When testimony is offered for the record, the psychiatrist must try to be aware of the legislator's hidden agenda. For instance, rather than looking at the open hearing solely as a means of becoming informed on a given subject by an expert, the legislator may view the hearing as an exercise, a gesture toward democracy, and may consequently ignore the speaker and the subject entirely. Many legislators, however, will take advantage of the opportunity to use the record to benefit their particular cause. This may involve appearing rigorous because the voter perceives them as being too passive, or taking a stand on some issue that will help in current or future political battles.

While legislators may hope to achieve many objectives through a hearing, an overriding objective is to get information. The psychiatrist's presentation should anticipate and respond to the legislator's principal policy-making concerns and recognize the area he serves. In this instance, they are concerned with the type, cost, extent and effectiveness of services that people want and need. Dr. Dodd's answers to specific questions should have addressed these broader issues so that the legislators understand what the psychiatrist is advocating.

The commentators agree that the most effective way to make a point clear is to offer concrete evidence and data whenever possible. This includes the careful choice of examples and data which illustrate the need for mental health care and, wherever possible, provide reference point information and illustrative cases from the legislator's own constituency. Congressional aides have generally researched the speaker's basic opinions and have a good idea of what is going to be said in an open hearing. It is the speaker's challenge to support his/her comments intelligently, and to offer specific proposals for governmental action.

The psychiatrist should state his opinions firmly, but this should not preclude a willingness to compromise. Legislators will respond to compelling arguments and attempt to work with the speaker, but they may be constrained by governmental and political realities and responsibilities. In taking the initiative, the psychiatrist can suggest congressional actions and simultaneously offer alternatives, substantial information and areas of possible compromise.

Dr. Dodd's dialogue raised some key issues in mental health programming, such as allocation of resources in the face of shrinking funds, the question of who should pay for services, effectiveness of treatment, the role of the community mental health center, and the issue of comprehensive health care coverage versus categorical funding for mental health programs. However, he failed to set direction or priorities among these issues because his presentation and his responses to questions were insufficiently focused. For example, Dr. Dodd did not offer a plan of action for the expansion of the Title XX program so that it would alleviate pressures on mental health funding, nor did he take the opportunity to discuss the Child Health Assessment Program, when the issue came up. When proposing that the problems with deinstitutionalization be publicized to ensure additional funding sources for patients' housing and social service needs, Dr. Dodd failed to ask for congressional help. With greater preparation, he could have responded to the question of the effectiveness of treatment by supplying the legislators with summaries of specific studies related to treatment evaluation, then pointing out the limitations and expense involved in preparing these analyses. In this dialogue, the psychiatrist's wide-ranging discourse prevented an in-depth pursuit of the issues.

Point of View: Psychiatry

The psychiatrists' response to Dr. Dodd's dialogue with the Senate Committee overlapped that of the non-medical professionals. The psychiatric commentators felt that a psychiatrist addressing a congressional hearing should be prepared to face a well-educated, aggressive group.

Psychiatrists must recognize that many of the questions that Congressmen have asked of them in past exchanges have remained unanswered, accounting for some skepticism about the mental health field. In addition, legislators will respond according to their particular notions of the concept of mental illness.

Hesitant to accept a very comprehensive definition of mental illness, the Senators in the dialogue tried to discriminate between the "serious mental illness" and the "social service" domains. While the Senators acknowledged the need for community mental health centers to focus their attention on helping the deinstitutionalized psychiatric patient, they confronted Dr. Dodd on the lack of services for children and the elderly. Had Dr. Dodd chosen to advocate the need for *comprehensive* mental health care, he might have suggested a system by which this would be possible, pointing out the inadequacies of the current system and the need for ancillary services within the mental health network. Conversely, had Dr. Dodd decided to advocate *limited* responsibility for community mental health centers, he could have proposed plans by which alternative agencies and programs would pick up the additional service demands.

If Dr. Dodd had anticipated Senator Alpert's desire for definable goals and quantifiable needs for mental health care, he could have responded more effectively to the question about the treatment of smoking. If psychiatrists have a difficult time agreeing on which treatment is essential for a patient's condition, it is understandable that legislators, unaware of the complexity of diagnosis and the alternative treatment modalities, have trouble accepting these controversies. Looking for "hard" treatment decisions and effective and permanent results from therapy, Senators are understandably suspicious of the inclusion of smoking as a disorder. They then question the credibility of the psychiatrists' definition (the DSM working definition) of mental disorder and the public's role in blindly financing endless and limitless psychiatric work.

Claiming no expertise in the field of smoking research, Dr. Dodd wisely chose not to convince the Committee that smoking is a mental illness which should be treated, but he could have confronted the legislators' concerns squarely, nonetheless. Dr. Dodd could have explained the more general purposes of DSM III, and some of the difficulties in diagnosing disorders, etc. At the same time, he could have assured the Senators that psychiatrists would be willing to work toward a flexible use of diagnostic categories which address both patient care and cost considerations. Proposing that the legislators, rather than mental health professionals, make the decision with respect to which mental illnesses should have treatment paid for by insurance recognizes the reality of who holds the purse strings. However, the language Dr. Dodd used provided evidence for the legislators that the whole system of determining degrees of mental illness is arbitrary.

The psychiatrist commentators also brought up the issue of treatment effectiveness. A psychiatrist should anticipate this question and respond by explaining the difficulties of evaluating treatment effectiveness by providing examples of studies which have been undertaken, and by explaining the costs involved in evaluation.

The role of the psychiatrist in the mental health field and, specifically, within the community mental health center is an area of confusion for legislators. Dr. Dodd should have first examined his own beliefs about the proper role of the psychiatrist in mental health care programs and then presented that view consistently. Instead, he avoided the issue when he proposed that psychiatrists should direct mental health programs without stating why this should be so.

Legislators often perceive psychiatrists as requiring payment for their own services at the expense of reimbursing other mental health workers, professional or non-professional. This raises the question of the psychiatrist's role and function in relation to needed services provided by non-psychiatrists. In responding to this question, the psychiatrist has several choices. If he or she chooses to advocate a medical model, a case must be made to first explain why psychiatrists alone are especially capable of providing therapy, and how those services outside the psychiatric domain will be financed. If the psychiatrist chooses to advocate a community mental health model, he or she must be prepared to discuss the continuity and comprehensiveness of services. Specific information helps to decrease the Senators' suspicions of the psychiatrist's desire for hegemony in the mental health field.

Discussion

The dialogue between Dr. Dodd and the Senate Committee is best perceived as an exercise in interpretation and anticipation of legislators' agenda. Our intent in this section is to summarize and capsulize the commentators' major points while adding our own recommendations. These comments may well be applicable to state and local bodies. To make effective use of the opportunity to present testimony before a legislative committee, the psychiatrist must first understand the nature of the forum. In order to anticipate the legislator's underlying assumptions about the particular case in question and the mental health field in general, he must also develop a strategy that permits optimal education and persuasion of the committee members.

The psychiatrist must be familiar with the purpose and composition of the legislative forum when preparing testimony since this will dictate the type, amount and focus of the material to be presented. A committee hearing is only one part of the much more complex legislative process.

During hearings, the psychiatrist should be aware of three things. 1) Congressmen may be variously motivated to provoke, rebuke or even ignore legislative testimony; their particular rationale for doing so will form the direction and ultimate use of the dialogue. 2) If the psychiatrist is drilled aggressively or ignored completely by the questioning legislators, he/she should not feel that this behavior is intended as a personal affront. 3) Both the legislator and the psychiatrist are trying to build a meaningful and useful record.

The witness at a congressional hearing is presumed to be an expert, but this does not mean that he/she knows everything However, the psychiatrist should be conversant with the pertinent facts and illustrations which are essential to the case at hand. When unfamiliar material is encountered, the psychiatrist can provide the Senators with the information they are seeking subsequent to the hearing. To evade tough questions with verbal maneuvers, or to present personal conclusions as hard facts, does harm to the credibility of the psychiatrist's testimony.

Political and financial realities practically ensure senatorial resistance to the mental health cause. Legislators, as a general rule, are skeptical about the growing demands for more extensive mental health care. This is due, in part, to the lack of quantifiable measurements on the effectiveness of, and need for, treatment. The psychiatrist must be prepared to alleviate these legislative concerns by providing carefully documented information on cost-control, evaluation of program efficacy, need, etc.

Keeping all these elements of effective procedure in mind, the psychiatrist must be careful to organize his/her material so that a number of concise, clear and consistent points emerge from the dialogue. Before a good case can be made, priorities should be organized coherently. The psychiatrist may use a number of questions as guidelines in shaping testimony. For example: How complex or simple should the argument be? Should specific or general points be stressed? Where might relationships between constituency needs and programmatic plans be drawn? Is the psychiatrist acting as an individual, as a protagonist for a particular agency, or as a lobbyist for a broader, professional alliance? In answering these and other questions, the psychiatrist must determine his/her position on the larger issues of mental health care as they pertain to the legislator's concerns.

The psychiatrist is advised to keep issues clear, and to proceed logically from step to step in answering and redirecting questions. Mixing and linking the issues from the start diffused (and defused) Dr. Dodd's presentation.

Within the context of a legislative forum, questions directed at the psychiatrist-witness have multiple explicit and implicit origins. There is always a manifest question which the psychiatrist must decide either to answer or to deflect. Subsumed within it will likely be several latent questions. The psychiatrist must first determine how straightforward the inquiry is intended to be. Next, he/she must evaluate the breadth and depth of the Senator's concerns and calculate which question or questions to address. If cognizant of these, the psychiatrist can use his/her response to one or more of the questions to highlight points of the overall argument.

As stressed by the commentators, the use of examples, especially clinical examples, adds a personal and sympathetic dimension to the presentation of congressional testimony which is lacking in theoretical and abstract material. Examples can serve another important function as well. When judiciously selected, examples can be used to answer a number of questions at once.

The ability and ease with which a psychiatrist can respond to multiple agendas simultaneously—his or her own priorities and the legislator's challenges—will have direct bearing on the success of the legislative committee hearing. The psychiatrist should strive to synthesize the numerous factors which will shape the outcome and effectiveness of the legislative dialogue. It is the psychiatrist's responsibility to be aware of the implications of his or her testimony. In a broad sense, when speaking before a legislative committee, the witness, his or her expertise, and the discipline are all being examined.

9

**CONCLUSION
WHAT HAVE WE LEARNED?**

9

Conclusion
What Have We Learned?

Now that we have explored these various interfaces of psychiatry with others, and having drawn on the collective wisdom of participants on both sides, what have we learned?

First, we have learned that the most important challenge is to achieve *effective* mutual communication between persons of different orientation or background. That process sometimes is limited to the provision of rational information, at other times it involves persuasion, and at yet other times, it requires the exercise of authority.

For the non-psychiatrists, it is important to avoid stereotyping psychiatrists and psychiatric opinions. Not all psychiatrists are the same. If you encounter a psychiatrist with whom you are unable to communicate, first try to understand what is impeding communication, and if that fails look for another one with whom you can relate. Or, if you reach an impasse, find a consultant who may help overcome the stalemate. When you are confronted with psychiatric jargon or material which you cannot understand, ask for further definition and clarification. Make your questions and concerns as explicit as possible, and help the psychiatrist learn "your language."

For psychiatrists, it is important to develop a sensitivity to the different styles of communication of other decision-makers. Those who are psychiatrists may be most comfortable with the more clinical style of communication used daily in the treatment of patients. Quite different are the legal style (of equal adversaries), the political style (of unequal adversaries), and the pedagogical style (teacher-student). Psychiatrists also must redouble their efforts to measure what they are doing, and to identify objective criteria which will reflect outcome in terms that decision-makers can understand and use.

In the interests of achieving more effective communication in interfaces between psychiatrists and decision-makers outside of the mental health field, we offer to all groups, but especially to psychiatrists, the following 15 points which summarize much of the previous discussions.

Before the encounter:

1. Do your homework. Be as familiar as possible with the issues at hand and the answers you need to have.

2. Be conscious of the other person's circumstances—his values, his "language," his commitments—and respect them.

3. Be sensitive to the process of the interaction, especially the rules and practices of the specific situation in which you are involved.

4. Know your limits. Don't expect to be all things to all people. Use consultants or other resource persons who are familiar with the problem and the situation, and who can help you present your case.

During the encounter:

5. Identify mutual concerns and common goals of both parties. Seek to develop an alliance for the purpose of solving the problem.

6. Define the issue and stick with it. Don't digress.

7. Listen. Keep cool, and don't argue. (At times, noncommunication may be the best communication.)

Conclusion

8. Use simple language and concrete, familiar examples. Avoid technical jargon and difficult-to-understand abstract examples.

9. Don't bluff. Feel free to say frequently, "I don't know" and "I'll find out."

10. Keep your sense of humor but direct it at yourself, not at your questioner.

11. Keep your narcissism and self-righteousness in firm check.

12. Don't expect to win them all. At the point of impasse, back off and seek mediation.

After the encounter:

13. Remember that additional encounters probably will occur in the future. Review what happened and learn from it.

14. Do not leave unresolved issues until the next time. (Some of the most fruitful exchanges can take place at times other than when an encounter is in progress.)

15. Informed contacts and meetings with decision-makers should be encouraged. (Even if issues are not on the "agenda" or resolved, pathways for communication can be established by getting to know each other.)

ACKNOWLEDGMENTS TO CONTRIBUTORS

The program of the Group for the Advancement of Psychiatry, a nonprofit, tax exempt organization, is made possible largely through the voluntary contributions and efforts of its members. For their financial assistance during the past fiscal year in helping it to fulfill its aims, GAP is grateful to the following:

Abbott Laboratories
American Charitable Foundation
Dr. and Mrs. Jeffrey Aron
Dr. and Mrs. Richard Aron
Virginia & Nathan Bederman Foundation
Ciba Pharmaceutical Company
Maurice Falk Medical Fund
Geigy Pharmaceuticals
Mrs. Carol Gold
The Gralnick Foundation
The Grove Foundation
The Holzheimer Fund
The Island Foundation
Ittleson Foundation, Inc., for Blanche F. Ittleson Consultation Program
Marion E. Kenworthy-Sarah H. Swift Foundation, Inc.
Lederle Laboratories
McNeil Laboratories
Merck, Sharp & Dohme Laboratories
Merrell-National Laboratories
Phillips Foundation
Sandoz Pharmaceuticals
The Murray L. Silberstein Fund (Mrs. Allan H. Kalmus)
The Smith Kline Corp.
Mr. and Mrs. Herman Spertus
E.R. Squibb & Sons, Inc.
Jerome Stone Family Foundation
Tappanz Foundation
van Ameringen Foundation
Mr. S. Winn
Wyeth Laboratories

INDEX

A

Administrative costs, issue of, 124-126
Advocate. *See* Patient advocate
Allerton, W. S., 120

B

Barondess, J. A., 78
Bateman, J., 120
Behavior, outlooks on determinants of, 46-48, 51-52
Bibb, J. W., 120
Bourne, P. G., 138
Brooks, D., 40
Budget analyst
    analysis of interface with, 119-136
    dialogue with, 121-131
    discussion regarding, 134-136
    point of view of, 131-133

C

Campbell, R. J., 138
Chodoff, P., 56
Commitment
    issues in, 19-38
    temporary solution to, 37
Committee on Mental Health Services, 14
Communication
    with non-psychiatric physician, 87-88, 95-97
    with police officer, 31-33
    principles of, 95-97, 162-163
Community Mental Health Centers Act, 148
Community mental health programs
    and federal funding, 139-158
    psychiatrist's role in, 141-142
    and state funding, 121-136
Confidentiality, issue of, 44
Cutler, J., 138

D

Dangerousness, concepts of, 22-23, 31-32, 84-85
Deinstitutionalization, issue of, 143-144
Diagnosis, issues in, 58-60
DuVal, M. K., 78

E

Elderly, issue of, 144-145

F

Finley, J., 100
Friedman, P., 40
Funding level, issue of, 122-123

G

Gemelli, S. J., 18
Gibson, R. W., 100
Goldman, W., 120
Greenblatt, M., 40
Greenhill, M. H., 78
Guillette, W., 56

H

Hackett, T. P., 78
Halfway houses, issue of, 128-129

Health planner
  analysis of interface with, 99-117
  dialogue with, 101-108
  discussion regarding, 116-117
  point of view of, 108-113
Health Systems Agency (HSA)
  goals of, 109
  interface with, 99-117
Hospitalization, issues of, 70-72, 102-104
Hospitals, psychiatry in, 77-98
Hottenroth, T. M., 100
Hughett, B., 120

I

Insanity, issue of, 85-86
Insurance coverage
  issues of, 55-76
  overuse of, 65-66

J

Jones, R. E., 40
Jones, S. B., 138
Julian, R. E., 100

K

Kelly, N. K., 100
Kelly, P. E., 18
Klein, J. I., 40
Klerman, G. L., 138

L

Legislator
  analysis of interface with, 137-158
  dialogue with, 139-150
  discussion regarding, 156-158
  point of view of, 150-153
LeWinn, L. M., 40
Lipsitt, D. R., 78

M

McIntosh, C. P., 120
McNerney, W. J., 56
Medical records, issue of, 69
Medication, issue of, 45-46, 51;
  role of, 82-84
Mental health, public concern over, 13
Mental illness, severe, issue of, 139-141
Milt, J., 100
Modlin, H. C., 18
Morrill, R. G., 100

N

National Health Planning and Resources Development Act of 1974, 108, 148
National Institute of Mental Health, 146, 147
Newman, W., 100
Nover, R. A., 56

P

Patient advocate
  analysis of interface with, 39-54
  dialogue with, 41-48
  discussion of issues regarding, 52-54
  point of view of, 48-49
  role of, 42
Patient rights, issues in, 39-54
Penner, N. R., 56
Perlin, M. L., 40
Physicians, non-psychiatric
  analysis of interface with, 77-98
  dialogue with, 79-87
  discussion regarding, 97-98
  point of view of, 88-92
Police officer
  analysis of interface with, 17-38
  boundary of, 35-36

Index

dialogue with, 19-26
discussion regarding, 34-38
point of view of, 26-29
referral function of, 33-34
President's Commission on Mental Health, 140, 147
Psychiatry
  accountability viewpoint of, 133-134
  boundary of, 35-36
  and budget analysts, 119-136
  commitment viewpoint of, 29-34
  and communication, 31-33, 87-88, 95-97, 161-163
  congressional hearings viewpoint of, 153-155
  consultation role of, 80, 91-92
  counsel used by, 52-53
  educational role of, 31-32, 111
  and health planners, 99-117
  Health Systems Agency viewpoint of, 113-116
  hospital setting viewpoint of, 92-97
  and legislators, 137-158
  liaison role of, 93-95
  medical treatment compared with, 73, 88-90
  mutual problem identification by, 74-75
  and non-psychiatric physicians, 77-98
  and patient advocate, 39-54
  patient's rights viewpoint of, 50-52
  and police officers, 17-38
  preventive, issue of, 63-64
  publics of, 13-15
  recommendations to, in dealings with attorneys, 53-54
  rehabilitation viewpoint of 70-72
  and third-party payors, 55-76

R

Rappeport, J. B., 18
Richman, A., 56

S

Sadoff, R. L., 18
Schizophrenia, latent, 60-62
Sharfstein, S. S., 56
Shore, M. F., 40
Smucker, R. M., 138
Stolberg-Acosta, R., 40
Stone, A. A., 18

T

Third-party payor
  analysis of interface with, 55-76
  and community mental health programs, 124
  and concurrent review, 75
  and day hospitals, 106-107
  dialogue with, 57-67
  discussion regarding, 72-76
  and national health insurance, 145-146
  point of view of, 67-69
  responsibilities of, 73-74
Treatment alternatives
  day hospital and inpatient care as, 105-106
  and health planners, 99-117

W

Winslade, W. J., 40

NO LONGER THE PROPERTY
OF THE
UNIVERSITY OF R.I. LIBRARY